Advanced Praise
for *On and Off the Couch*

On And Off The Couch is a beautifully written love letter to psychoanalysis and its power to transform a life. Kolsky gives us an insider's look into her own journey of becoming free and independent as a woman, and as a psychoanalyst. This compelling memoir reveals the author's devotion to her patients, the lucky beneficiaries of her own self exploration. We are fortunate that she found her voice, one worth listening to.

—Lisa Sokoloff, MSW, LCSW, PsyA, Supervisor and Instructor IPS

Pure Gold! Kolsky offers a profound universal remedy that highlights the vital force of psychoanalysis and brilliantly opens the gateway to the intricate world of inner reality. In today's complex world, *On and Off the Couch: Memoir of a Psychoanalyst* demonstrates the value of introspection in order to establish the equilibrium necessary to keep one afloat on the river of life.

—Nuzhat Nada, Instructor, Human Development/Psychology

On and Off the Couch illuminates the complex process of psychoanalysis, its goals, challenges, and benefits, as the author tells of her personal experience on both sides of the process. Using clear and easily understandable language, Kolsky also clarifies the differences between other forms of psychotherapy and counselling. Readers who have been practitioners of psychotherapy, those who have experienced therapy, as well as those who are students in the field of mental health, will find this an interesting, informative and engaging book.

—Ginny B. Schwartz, Ph.D., Former Director of Counselling Services,
St. Lawrence University

Kolsky's memoir is one woman's odyssey illustrating the best uses of psychoanalysis. Beginning in the conflicted regions of youth, it culminates in a snowy and contented walk in the woods in a maturity framed by psychoanalysis' insights.

—Rosemary Steinbaum, Founding Trustee,
The Philip Roth Personal Library, Newark, N.J.

Here is a book that gracefully unravels the complex field of psychoanalysis. In Kolsky's stirring memoir, she smoothly intertwines her own experience of being psychoanalyzed with her later experience as a professional psychoanalyst. With perspectives from both on and off the couch, we are led to a deeper understanding of how the practice works and why it helps.

—Caperton Tissot, author, *History Between the Lines*
and other publications

ON AND OFF THE COUCH

ON AND OFF THE COUCH
Memoir of a Psychoanalyst

Beverly Kolsky, MSW, LCSW, BCD-P

International Psychoanalytic Books (IPBooks)
New York · http://www.IPBooks.net

ON AND OFF THE COUCH

Published by IPBooks, Queens, NY
Online at: www.IPBooks.net

ISBN: 978-1-956864-15-1

For Neil

Table of Contents

INTRODUCTION

I am about to gently lift the shroud that covers the field of psychoanalysis and its mysteries. Some of my colleagues may strongly disapprove of what I have to say about our profession. Patients may think they recognize themselves in my discussion of certain issues even though I have gotten their permission to take their stories and have taken great pains to disguise their identity, thus keeping the pact of confidentiality that is an essential aspect of the relationship between analyst and patient.

Finally, even members of my own family may be surprised and possibly stunned at the revelation of so many things that they have not known about me. Working as any kind of psychotherapist—and a psychoanalyst is a form of therapist—is in some ways like being a Secret Agent. We must keep secrets. We must inhabit a world where no one else can go except the patient we are analyzing.

I have worked as a psychotherapist for the past fifty years and began my own psychoanalysis in 1977. Although I have been partially retired since 2019, I still continue to see patients. In 1967, I graduated with a master's degree in social work from New York University Graduate School of Social Work, but not until five years later did I begin to work in the field and quickly realized that if I were to help people change their lives, I needed to understand more about my own.

I therefore began my own psychoanalyses and continued for a total of seventeen years working with two different analysts on two different continents who had two different theoretical approaches. Wanting to learn still more, in 1984 I began my first training at a psychoanalytic institute in

England, the setting in which analysts are traditionally trained. But because I returned to the States in 1986, I completed my training at The New York Institute for Psychoanalytic Self Psychology in New York City in 2006.

What follows is the story of my life before and after being psychoanalyzed. I also tell the stories of a few of my patients, obtaining their permission and disguising gender and many other details to preserve patient privacy. This pact of confidentiality is an essential aspect of the relationship between analyst and patient.By doing so, I hope to increase understanding of one of the most intimate and controversial relationships in the field of health. I also hope to show how, when, and why psychoanalysis and psychoanalytic psychotherapy, another form of depth psychology, really work.

In the last half century, the field, wreathed in mystery to begin with, has become even more mysterious, because it has undergone so many changes. These changes raise new questions, such as who now is practicing psychoanalysis, which of the many theoretical approaches in the field are they using, and how well do they work?

People typically have other questions about psychoanalysis. "Do I need to lie on the couch?" "How often should I go?" And inevitably, always, "Why is psychoanalysis so expensive?" (Although fees vary considerably among analysts and can be adjusted according to the experience of the analyst and the financial situation of the patient, they can go as high as $350 for a forty-five-minute "hour" and even higher in big cities.)

And they also wonder: Does analysis help? Do dreams really have meaning? Is there really an unconscious and if so why is it so important? What is this "inner world" psychoanalysts talk about and do I really have one?" And finally, what is psychoanalysis and how is it different from psychotherapy and counselling?

* * *

I became intrigued by the idea of psychoanalysis in the New York City of the 1960's. I was in my mid-twenties, living in Brooklyn Heights with my first husband and attending graduate school in social work. In my second, rigorous year of training, I was an intern at a psychiatric hospital in which a variety of treatments were being given to inpatients, including electric shock therapy. But the foundation, by which these treatments were measured, was a psychoanalytic one. The ghost of Sigmund Freud peered down at us, hovered around us, no matter how much family therapy or group therapy or medications were being given.

In addition, so many members of my generation were being psychoanalyzed, or thinking about being psychoanalyzed, or discussing it, or wondering if they "needed it." Board games like *Group Therapy* described as being "For people who want to open up. Get in touch. Let go. Feel free," were being played in marijuana-scented living rooms while Ravi Shankar competed with the Beatles as background music.

Young women ringed their eyes with kohl and wore mini-skirts that revealed a part of the leg rarely before seen in public. (Older women and widows often dressed in black, were said to make the sign of the cross when they passed those girls in the streets.) The men who accompanied these young women typically wore jeans, sandals, and black turtlenecks, sometimes with velvet jackets, and their hair was often as long as a girl's.

For women, long, bone-straight hair was the fashion, preferably framing their faces like curtains "Mama Cass" style. I had my wavy black hair straightened at Kenneth's, the upscale salon just off Fifth Avenue on the Upper East Side of Manhattan where Jackie Kennedy famously acquired her signature bouffant. I was younger than Jackie would have been, a fashionable Beatles lover whose mind was on more serious things than hair length, but I went nevertheless.

I and other members of my generation were searching for something elusive. Swept up by the Sixties, we were serious about trying to find answers to concerns that the Baby Boomers were voicing, such as war and peace, serenity and love, nirvana. Regardless of what we had, we hungered for more, but the hunger was of a spiritual nature. We wanted to know the meaning of life. We asked philosophical questions and looked for answers in books, fiction and non-fiction, in philosophy and psychology, and of course in psychedelic drugs. We wanted to live fully and that meant knowing the mind and its functions as well as our sexual bodies. We searched for union in whatever way we could experience it and for however long it took to find it. We were a new breed of youth.

Then as now, it was generally thought that to be psychoanalyzed was to be "elitist." It was thought that only rich people or liberals or intellectuals had the desire to "navel gaze." That part of the reputation of psychoanalysis remains, despite the fact that the field has changed drastically since the 1960's. Today some psychoanalysts ply their trade to patients who come for once-a-week (or even less frequent) therapy, whereas patients used to come three to five times per week. People come for advice on how to get along with their mother-in-law or what to do about a difficult boss instead of coming because they want to change themselves.

Although a couch can be found in every psychoanalyst's office, it is more frequently used for sitting on rather than for lying down. Long before the coronavirus pandemic that arrived in the United States in early 2020, analyst and patient gazed freely at one another. Now this has become the norm as virtual apps like Zoom and FaceTime have by necessity replaced person-to-person sessions in an office.

* * *

I believe that one of the major reasons for the change is because analysts no longer need a medical degree to get further training. Since 1978, psychoanalytic training has opened its doors to other candidates, people pulled from professions like social work, psychology, teaching and theology. And the professions that they come from may inadvertently color and inform their work just as a medical model underpinned that of Sigmund Freud, the Austrian neurologist who was the giant of the field. My first psychoanalyst had a literary background. My second, had been an actor. I can still hear his voice resonate when he wanted to make a point.

Of course, psychoanalysis as it was conceived by Freud, in which the analyst act as a "blank screen," still exists in its original form. Historically the analyst was a shadowy figure who, as if enclosed in an invisible confessional, also sat out of sight of the patient, listening for free associations, the uncensored monologues from which interpretations are made, and which were considered to be the heart of analysis. The analyst gave neither advice nor reassurance, nor did he express love for the patient.

This was so because psychoanalysis was considered to be a science. Like medicine, the patient was expected to conform to an already existing diagnosis or theory, and treatment followed from there. Today, in contemporary psychoanalysis, many analysts are far less rigid and combine theory with intuition. They practice the art of being in a two-person relationship with the patient. For example, self-disclosure on the part of the analyst, who might reveal aspects of himself and his feelings deriving from that relationship, is becoming an acceptable theoretical practice. This approach is called Relational Psychoanalysis.

Fathered by Freud, psychoanalytic theory has engendered many differing theories that also aim for in-depth treatment but use other theoretical approaches to get there. Heinz Kohut and his theory of self psychology is one, as are the theories of Carl Jung who founded analytical psychology. Donald Winnicott, Carl Rogers, and Michael Fairbairn are just a few of the names associated with the school of object relations which emphasizes working with internalized objects (significant others like a mother) and other phenomena in the inner world of early childhood. The list is endless. The aim is the same:

self-discovery, self-understanding and the easing of symptoms that hinder a person's ability to function in the world.

The changing face of health insurance and the skyrocketing cost of medical care also have a huge impact on the way psychotherapy is practiced. Generally, insurance companies prefer short-term and behavioral-based therapies to once or sometimes twice per week sessions. Preference is also given to the use of psychotropic drugs such as Lexapro, Effexor, Zoloft, and Prozac. Not only do insurance companies find this less costly, but many psychiatrists are choosing to become psychopharmacologists rather than endure the lengthy and costly training that becoming a certified psychoanalyst entails.

* * *

The greatest source of confusion in the field of psychotherapy, however, involves terminology. The word itself has become an umbrella term for all forms of talk therapy. Psychoanalysis is a type of psychotherapy. Both treat mental and emotional disorders. There is also something called psychoanalytic psychotherapy, a discipline that lies somewhere between the two fields. But only in psychoanalysis and in psychoanalytic psychotherapy is the aim to delve as deeply as possible into the core of one's self. Psychoanalysis, and by extension psychoanalytic psychotherapy, does this by encouraging the patient to talk freely about personal experiences, early childhood, and dreams, whereas most other forms of therapy do not.

At the other end of the psychotherapy spectrum is counseling which addresses issues more at their surface—for example, how to stop drinking, without exploring the deeper reasons why a person has become an alcoholic in the first place. If a person wants only to stop drinking there are methods available by which to do so notably through organizations like Alcoholics

Anonymous. If a person wants to understand the need to drink, a deeper psychotherapy is required. Understanding why something happens makes it easier to be in control of that behavior and thus engenders real and lasting change.

Still other options are available for the person who needs help changing a particular behavior, among them are: group therapy, marital therapy, couples therapy, behavior modification therapy, and cognitive behavioral therapy. The goal of these approaches is to eliminate symptoms without necessarily helping the patient to understand why the symptoms are there. As in counseling, there are usually specific techniques applied in addition to talking. However, particularly in marital and group therapy, patients can often move on into individual treatment to understand themselves at a deeper level.

* * *

Although psychoanalysts often have a string of letters after their names on their business cards to indicate that they have advanced training, I have found that very few people know what they stand for. Words like psychotherapy or counseling have become catch-all terms to anyone going for help, but they represent different levels of training and education. That is all fine. But if anyone looking for a therapist is lucky enough to find someone who has received special training as a psychoanalyst, that patient will be in the best possible place to find the kind of help being hoped and searched for.

This is so because psychoanalysts are required to undergo their own personal analysis before entering the psychoanalytic field. Because self-awareness is a crucial ingredient in helping other people develop theirs, not requiring other psychotherapists to have had their own therapy is, in my opinion, a glaring and dangerous omission. It was by undergoing my psychoanalysis that I came to both know myself and learn and understand what the process involves.

* * *

What does remain despite all these changes is that the heart of psychoanalysis involves digging deeply into the psyche to obtain an understanding of one's self, and by extension, other people. Such an understanding makes life easier. It simply does. It helps acquire clarity not only about ourselves but also about others and, yes, about the way the world works. This knowledge in turn helps us better place ourselves in it. Because we know more about our own needs, we are better able to place ourselves in the world. Because we know more about our own needs, we are able to situate ourselves in a place where those needs have a chance at being met.

We are in a position to know good from evil and, right from wrong, without judgment or prejudice. By coming to know our inner world, which is made up of thoughts that we would not utter to one another, fears that we cannot name, anger that has no tangible target, and the unconscious which by definition we cannot know until we work to reveal it, we honor our own truth. In doing so, we come to know greater truths.

A word about evil. That evil exists is one of these truths. If we are to fight evil, we cannot deceive ourselves about it. To bring change into the outer world we must first understand our inner one. The maxim, "know thyself" has never been truer. As the world spins out its disasters like Covid 19, climate change, economic and racial upheaval, we learn that the only thing we might be able to know is ourselves.

By writing this book and laying bare the underpinnings of how psychotherapy works and how it can help a person, I hope that some readers who have been thinking about going into therapy (analytic or otherwise) will be able to take that leap, or at least have a clearer understanding of the way the process works. That process can be very challenging at times, especially as the lies one tells one's self are being unraveled. But that is for both the individual's good and the greater good.

One of the most common criticisms of psychoanalysis has been that it creates dependence on the analyst and does not lead to change despite the fact that analysis can go on for many years. My personal and professional experience has been just the opposite. It has been by understanding my inner world that the outer one became clarified. I have moved from being a silent observer of life while living on the fringe, to becoming a person both engaged with its beauty and its ugliness, and still my heart brims with love — at least most of the time.

In times like these where one's very existence is threatened by viruses that can kill and lies that are told as truths, it is essential that people know their own truth. I have seen this kind of transformation happen in my patients also. As they near the end of their treatment and possess a deeper understanding of themselves and those around them, they are able to feel love and express true commitment in a more discriminating but satisfying fashion.

I say all this humbly. It took years, even decades, to acquire this knowledge. I want to pass it on to you.

PART ONE:

LOOKING FOR LIFE IN ALL THE WRONG PLACES:

THE PRE-ANALYTIC QUEST

CHAPTER ONE

LOST

Being lost takes many forms. The most insidious is not knowing that one is lost. And that was me, as my husband and I boarded the SS France in October of 1967.

I was full of excitement for the trip ahead, my first to Europe. Streamers were thrown from the ship's railings, confetti flew round our heads, and horns were blasting as we walked up the gang plank with an entourage of family bidding us good-bye. I, dressed in a black crepe low-waisted sheath dress with my long dark hair flowing, felt like an Italian film star. In fact, I had recently watched a black and white Italian film in which a young woman returns to her small Italian village after becoming famous, and walks up the cobbled narrow street to cheers and applause from her family and neighbors hanging over the balconies to welcome her back. My husband looked my counterpart with his long, straight, jet black hair and intense dark eyes. Slim and dark-complexioned, exotic-looking and attractive, we made a fine-looking young couple. Once we reached our cabin, champagne corks popped amidst hugs and good wishes for a "bon voyage." I remember shouting out to my father-in-law above the noisy crowd, that all would be well, having noticed that he looked worried and had a slightly disapproving expression on his face. We were going to Europe for an indefinite period of time, travelling wherever we liked, with no restrictions. I was euphoric with a sense of adventure.

It was not that I felt a need for adventure, or for anything specific. I had just completed graduate school. I was not feeling that I had to get away from anything or that I had anything harmful in my life. There was nothing "bad" to feel encumbered by. I wanted something that I could not name. It was easier to identify a desire for something to come my way that would fill it perfectly. Passively I waited, peering down that road along which many things were headed towards me.

The odd thing was that when something did come my way, something I would have liked, I refused it. For example, I have always liked to sing. As a child, I sang my way through lead roles in summer camp musicals, and in high school choir, and college get-togethers with musician friends. But on a day in 1966 while I was shopping at Bloomingdale's for my husband's twenty-sixth birthday present, and a young man approached me asking me if I sang, I abruptly replied, "No." He persisted, explaining that he was forming a folk music group and that I looked perfect for one of the singing parts. He had a quiet and sincere manner about him, and the card that he gave me confirmed his position. Nonetheless I shook my head and looked away until he left me to continue sorting through men's shirts.

I have remembered this man over the years whenever I have thought about missed opportunities and unrealized potential. It was out of fright that I refused him. I was shy, introverted, afraid of being the center of attention even though in truth I would probably have liked that a lot. It was a fear of having what I wished for, if I could have even, allowed myself to have wishes. Hoping for something rather than possessing it kept fantasy alive and fantasy was preferable to reality because reality brought with it, fear.

I knew only that each time I found something I thought to be precious, I realized that the need for something truly meaningful was still there. That which felt familiar to me was a state of longing, along with the hope that I

14

would find something that belonged to me, something that was waiting for me to claim as mine.

This emotional state made me an easy prey for falling in love. To be recognized by something outside of myself, to be seen by another as I would like to be seen was an aphrodisiac, a drug that elated me and then disappointed me. It was only after the party was over, the laughter had worn off, the money had run out, when the other woman suddenly appeared and slapped my face, when these things happened again and again, that I realized that I had found nothing. But this epiphany was long in coming. Before that, the cycle was repeated over and over. Periodically I became exhausted, limp, tarnished, and each time, more profoundly lost.

Years later when I sought therapy and was living on my own in England, I felt disconnected from these tumultuous emotions. I was not conscious of the fact that my relationships were an issue for me. I had always rebounded from the falls so that I continued to think that I was fine and that life was full of possibilities. As I was working as a therapist in London, I had rationalized that I needed therapy so that I could experience what I was giving. It was only right, I thought, to know firsthand what I was to be giving out. And so it is. Fortunately, this rationalization began my journey into realizing how lost I had been.

* * *

I threw away my first husband like a fisherman throwing a dead fish back into the sea. We were living on the island of Hydra in Greece at the time. True, he had betrayed me by having a weekend tryst with another woman. Although this was unlike him and it caught me by surprise, I knew that our sexual relationship, once we married, was an uneasy one for both of us. We never discussed it or let on to each other that this was so. I think we both felt, or at least I did, that I did not know how to fix it anyway so what was there to talk about? And was there anything to talk about? I had heard that the first year of marriage is the most difficult in adjusting to each other but when it continued into the next four and all during this time we were such good friends, I accepted it; or I thought that I had; or I thought that he had. When he guiltily told me about the betrayal on the day of his return, I could feel my heart break with a sense of my own failure. It did not matter that he begged me to stay with him, or that we were living a charmed life, or that we were soul mates. What mattered was that our marriage was not a marriage; and because of that, it failed.

I did not consciously know that then. I knew nothing. I was twenty-five years old and he was a year older. But I think now, that neither one of us was ready for the commitment that marriage demands. We had gotten married with the idea that a marriage could be whatever a couple made it to be. Yes, we were married in a synagogue, but it was The Brotherhood Synagogue in Greenwich Village. That great building that seated so many, hosted that day the two of us, my mother, his parents and a cleaning lady who wandered in at the time of the brief ceremony and sat down in the back pew. Siblings, friends, extended family were excluded as we thought that would make our union seem too conventional. Certainly while we courted, our physical relationship had been a good one. But somehow marriage had dampened our ardor. I felt that something was wrong, but I didn't know why or what exactly. I wanted more, but not as in the words of the song, "Is that all there is?" Rather, I asked myself, "Is this what marriage is?"

A few weeks after my husband's announcement of his infidelity, like a plant moving towards the light, I fell in love with another man. We were still living on the Greek island of Hydra where we had travelled expressly so that my husband could make the acquaintance of Leonard Cohen, the singer-songwriter who was living on this tiny outpost in the Aegean Sea. It was the winter of 1968. Our mornings usually took us into the port where we picked up our mail and stopped at the taverna for Turkish coffee and chats with Leonard, along with a few other foreigners living on the island. There were no cars on Hydra, nor even roads. Donkeys and people walked up and down the steep paths ringing the port which was flecked with uneven rows of whitewashed houses trimmed with blue shutters and blue doors. These dwellings were tucked higgledy-piggledy amongst the narrow uneven stone paths that led outwards from the central thoroughfare, wide enough for one man and one donkey. Nor was there electricity in most of these residences, and no running water.

But there was light, abundant light, celestial light. It penetrated the surface of things to make them appear mythical. It brought the artists and the melancholy to the island. It could, and did, bring change to people who arrived on Hydra to experience its legendary qualities. I remember one American woman who had set up a home on Hydra because the light, especially at sundown, helped her to feel less depressed about her daughter's suicide some years before. She often invited my husband and me, who were probably about the age that her daughter would have been, to have a drink with her at sunset to toast her daughter's memory.

As we entered the taverna one bright winter's day soon after my husband's confession, I felt a burning gaze directed at me and turned to see where it was coming from. In the corner of the room sat a man staring at me as if he had never seen such a vision before. His gaze was severe and relentless as though I were looking into a mirror lit by the sun. Sitting alone at the table as he was when I first saw him, I sensed danger. He was small in stature, blonde-haired with the lined and rugged face of an older man, but the body of a slender, muscular young one. The contrasts fascinated me. He looked worn but forceful, sensitive but tough, and very French with his tightly knit wiry body and casually stylish attire. He oozed sensuality. I tried to look away but I could not. He was fixing me with his eyes, possessing me, claiming me as though he had been waiting for me to walk through that door. I was suddenly frightened and wanted to escape through the sun-bleached doors of the building. But I could not will myself to move. I saw only the deep blue of his eyes pinning me to that moment. He was to become my sun; and I was to burn away years of my life in wanting to be close to him. In that instant, I thought that I had found all that I was looking for.

Jean Claude and I did not meet again until it was my turn, several weeks after my husband's confession, to spend the weekend away from Hydra. I had not much more to say to my husband as he only kept repeating how sorry he was. I felt uncomfortable around him and his guilty feelings; so I went to Athens, a two hour ferry ride from Hydra, with my friend Jenny. She was an Englishwoman whom I had also met that winter; and she had been invited to Jean Claude's flat in Athens for dinner. I learned from her that Jean Claude was forty-one years old, an excellent amateur painter of abstract impressionism; and that he stayed on Hydra to paint, but lived in Athens in order to sell his paintings. She said that he was charming. She insisted that I come along with her. I did, and I remained with him that night and for the next five years.

A day in the life of being lost can be as beautiful as any other day, or as lonely. This is especially true when one discounts where one has come from. When the past is non-existent because the present is all-consuming, we can be in trouble. Our past history must come with us. I knew none of that. Caught like the proverbial fly in a spider's web, I could not tear myself away from him, the moment, that present. Here was someone who saw me as I wanted to be seen. I felt special, womanly, beautiful.

* * *

So a month later as winter approached and Jean Claude moved back again to his Athens flat I went, too. When I knew that I could never return to my husband after being with Jean Claude, I leased the flat underneath his. We lived there for the rest of that winter, under the shadow of the Acropolis, separated by a ceiling during the day and by nothing every night.

The thick stone walls of the building where we lived trapped the cold in winter. There was no form of heat except in Jean Claude's flat, where he had a small upright gas heater that I could hover over when I was there. Alone in my own flat, after I had put on the few pieces of clothing that I had, a black velour dress, purple suede high boots and several shawls that I had recently bought in the Plaka, the marketplace beneath the Acropolis, I drank cup after cup of hot tea. When those efforts to keep warm failed, I reluctantly left the safety of my flat to cross the wide boulevard called Dionysiou Areropagitou.

The street climbed a hill that led away from Athens, or if followed downhill, it led into the center of Athens. I never wandered that far down or up; but I took daily walks crossing the quiet street to the ruins of the Acropolis, where the sun was strong enough to warm me in the open air. Jean Claude left for "work" on many of those days. This meant trying to show and to sell his paintings, which he was loathe to do. He seemed to be embarrassed by them as if they were never good enough, and compensated with his charm and powers of seduction. I wonder now if not only were his paintings for sale, but he was as well. Summoned to the homes of rich ladies who might want to buy a painting from him, there were always long lunches and much socializing which often ran into the evening. I never knew when he would return.

I was waiting, lingering on that broad plain of crumbling limestone that was the Acropolis. Waiting for Jean Claude to return. Waiting for a rescue from the despair that I felt about my marriage ending abruptly after my husband's infidelity, waiting in those ruins for a new life to begin. But I knew even then that there would be no rescue. Jean Claude professed to loathe the idea of marriage and children and offered neither. He had money enough to pay his rent most months, but nothing more. I had a small inheritance, a gift from my mother when I married. Life in Greece was cheap, but even I knew that this arrangement would not last forever. Rather than make choices according to reason, I ignored this obvious information. I surrendered completely to Jean Claude.

Climbing to the top of the worn stairs that led up from the street, the sight of the Acropolis always startled me. A flat plain strewn with chunks of marble and limestone with high decomposing columns rising above them, the scene resembled one in which children had been playing the game of statues, whirling in ever faster circles, arms clutching arms, spinning, spinning, until centrifugal force threw them apart, landing them in random frozen poses. I wandered slowly among these ancient rocks, sitting on some to catch the sun on my face, contemplating others to see what I could read from them. I never saw another person there, perhaps because it was winter. It therefore became easy for me to imagine that this curious plot of earth was mine alone and that these roofless, glassless, and doorless chambers were my waiting rooms. Below me I could hear the muffled sound of the city. Around me was the scent of eucalyptus trees fragrant in the crisp air. This was my garden, my home. If I stayed still long enough, I would know what I must do. If I were quiet enough, Jean Claude would keep me with him forever.

I thought of him in the city where he had gone mid-morning. He would be going to Kiffisia or some other rich section of Athens to have lunch with a well-off lady, bringing with him a few paintings hoping that she would want to buy one. I knew where he was. I had been to such places with my husband. In our travels to England we had met Greeks who were also studying Transcendental Meditation. They had taken a liking to us and invited us into their homes when they learned that we would be travelling to Athens, where we stayed for a few weeks before departing for Hydra. Most of them were very gracious aristocrats. We were fed sweets dripping with honey, served by maids in black uniforms with white lace collars. But after a while it seemed to us that our purpose in being there was to stave off the boredom of our hosts; and so we gave up the visits.

I never knew how Jean Claude knew these women. They materialized from a past life of his that I, of course, had not been a part of, but they hung over my head like an umbrella pock-marked with holes. From my perch on top of the hill, I liked to imagine that I could see him arriving at the carved wooden doors of a woman's home, a motley bunch of paintings under his arm. Envisioning a small man dwarfed by the tall heavy doors, I sensed his frustration as he jostled his burden with one hand while trying to free the other to ring the doorbell. He did not like to peddle his paintings. He did it at infrequent intervals, living from one sale till the next. Always there were huge abysses in between, which I carried him across by spending what was left of my inheritance.

It is painful for me now to relive how serenely I was living then. All that I could see was a beautiful man dressed for work, looking somewhat awkward in street clothes. He wore wide-wale tan corduroys and a V-neck sweater with a foulard tied around his neck. That and the mix of neutral colors set off by various touches of green gently blended together, declared his artist's eye. He always cut his own hair and wore it short, the blonde curls framing his face as Julius Caesar's had done.

When he painted or received guests in his flat, or when he received me, he wore a sprig of bougainvillea tucked behind one ear. This and a colorful sarong tied around his slim waist were often his only attire at home. With his muscular torso, he looked like the god Pan. With a wine carafe in one hand and a glass in the other, he morphed into Dionysius. With his tiny, highly arched feet and the way that his buttocks curved away from his back, he could have been a Centaur. And that is how I mostly thought of him. Half man, half beast, half devil, half angel, sacred and profane, a union of opposites that I could not fathom. He fascinated me. I continuously observed him, silently watching his every movement without him being aware of it.

He gave nothing away except his tenderness. He touched me, flirted with me, fed me food from his hands, kissing my mouth after every bite. He

21

tilted the wine glass to my lips and rushed back with it to catch the drops falling from my mouth. There were also times when the tenderness turned to teasing and then taunts. Seeing the bewilderment and hurt in my face, he would comfort me by wrapping my hands into both of his and holding them high in the air, shaking them as if they belonged to the rag doll that I had in that instant become. Cajoling me back into laughter and delight, I hardly recognized what had happened.

These things I knew of him: his love of Guerlain perfume that he dabbed onto himself every morning from nipples to crotch; his need for morning coffee, made strong in a clear glass pot and poured into big bowls, one for him and one for me with a croissant for dipping, followed by his first glass of wine for the day. And so his ritual of drinking three liters of wine a day would begin. I can see him even now pouring wine from a carafe, holding the stopper in the fist of his pouring hand, returning the carafe to the table and ceremoniously wiping the spilt drops with the fingers of that same hand still holding the stopper. To him, wine was the elixir necessary for living out his day. The only times when I saw him drunk were on the rare occasions, social evenings out, when whiskey or other spirits were added by our hosts to this base of daily wine consumption. Those times were ugly for me. He would flirt outrageously with any other woman who was present despite my sitting by his side. When the evening ended and, whether we were walking back to the flat in Paris or the house on Symi in Greece, I would gently reprimand him. But the fits of rage that were his reply quickly silenced me.

I also knew that he had attempted suicide by jumping out of a window when he was twenty-seven years old, thirteen years before I met him. Only once did he mention the episode to me and I knew that I could not ask more about it. He walked with a pronounced limp. One leg had become slightly shorter than the other, having never mended properly after the fall. He also told me once that he had had an incestuous relationship with his sister, Marie Rose. I knew to ask no more about that either. She came to visit us

22

periodically wearing magnificent clothes that she had made herself. One dress, I recall, had fifty cloth-covered buttons with tiny loopholes running down its back all laboriously made by her hand. Slim, quiet, modest, she seemed adoring of her older brother and was a benign, sporadic presence in our circle.

About Jean Claude's father, I knew slightly more than I did about the rest of his family. He told me that his father, who had held a position with the French government in Madagascar, had liked women and wine. There was one story about him that Jean Claude told repeatedly. During the war, the family returned to Paris from Madagascar where they all had been living. Food was in short supply in France. Father drove into the countryside where, he told his children, he would be fetching apples for them. The three young children were happy and excited to receive fresh food, given the privations of wartime, and they waited expectantly for him. When he returned, he took the apples from the trunk of the car and ceremoniously doused them with gasoline in front of his children. The apples were poisoned beyond use. The children continued to go hungry. There ends the story. Jean Claude would say nothing more. The tale always left me with a feeling of horror. Natural needs had not only been thwarted, but mutilated.

Jean Claude often had female visitors arrive at his flat unannounced. They were his friends with an intimation of having been past lovers. They welcomed me, exclaimed over me, and spoke of me in my presence as though I were a child who could not understand, even though they all spoke very careful and correct English. "Oh, but she looks so exotic. You must take her out. You must show her off. Why have you been hiding her?" They chattered and fussed over me while I listened in a state of wonder. Who were these ladies? Some of them were even younger than I. How did they get to be so sophisticated and sure of themselves?

Listening to them made me look at myself with a new respect. The hair that I had been told to straighten when I was married was now being given the freedom to hang loose and long and left to flow into its natural waves. My aquiline nose suddenly belonged to me and was not "just like her mother's." My white skin, black hair and blue eyes identified me as "black Irish" or English. If I was not quite one of them, I felt that I belonged with them, as if we were all part of a loving harem.

The feeling of being a part of something, of perhaps belonging somewhere, was eclipsed in the summer of 1970 when my money ran out. Jean Claude and I had been together for a period of about two years living between Athens, Paris, and a tiny village called Ouchamp, near the town of Blois in Loire et Cher. We had been lent a shepherd's cottage there that was due to undergo renovation. It belonged to his friend, Pierre, and had running water but no electricity, very low ceilings and was situated in a field by the side of a narrow country road. Across the road and up a little way, there was a farm, the only other dwelling within miles, where we walked or rode bicycles to get food supplies: chickens that were killed while we watched, newly made wine from grapes that we helped the farmers to harvest; snails fattened up in a wire enclosed box fixed to a post by the side of the road. These were the ingredients for gourmet meals that Jean Claude devised for us. He was an excellent cook and enjoyed making good, healthy food. Guests occasionally came from Paris, but mostly we were alone in that fall of 1968 when I decided that it was time to get a divorce.

My husband had stayed on in Europe travelling alone and asking me to meet up with him in the hope of a reconciliation. I gently refused and persistently asked for a divorce. It had been six or seven months since we separated. In desperation, he asked his parents to come to Europe to meet me, in order to see if they could persuade me to remain in the marriage. I agreed to meet them in London for the weekend; but I remained unmoved, and left after one night to return to Jean Claude in Paris. It was from there a few months later, in December of 1968, that I returned briefly to the United States to engage a lawyer who helped me to get a quick Mexican divorce.

Hastily I flew back to Paris after a short visit with my mother whom I had not seen since we sailed off in 1967. It was then that she told me that she was giving me no more advice or direction in my life because her having willed me into marriage had been a mistake. And after that, she never did advise me on anything. I was twenty-six years old.

* * *

In the first three years of our relationship, Jean Claude and I travelled back and forth between Greece and France. In Paris, he had a small maid's room in an attic in the Seventh Arrondissement given to him by a count and countess who lived below in a large flat. There was no bath or shower in this room under the eaves, but there was a small sink in the "kitchen" that doubled as his studio and a partition separating the single bed from the rest of this tiny space. The toilet, the kind that one squatted on, was in the narrow hallway and was shared with the daughter of the concierge, her husband and their two constantly crying infants. While I was solvent, I let a room with a shared bathroom in a small hotel nearby, but later when I was no longer, I stayed there with him.

In order to sell his paintings and to keep abreast of gallery and exhibition opportunities, Jean Claude had developed this arrangement; but I think it was more to return to Paris, to the French, where he seemed to feel most at home. He had always called himself an amateur painter as he had no formal training and relied for sales on word of mouth. The Count and Countess helped with introductions to people who might buy a painting from him. In some ways he was like their surrogate, a prodigal son living the bohemian life envied by that very correct, traditional couple. I was welcomed into their homes, both as an exotic American specimen, and as his well-enough-brought-up young mistress. His patrons and I respected, admired, and ogled each other through many long multi-coursed dinners.

In spite of these efforts, sales of Jean Claude's paintings were not frequent. After about seven more months of living in this way, I knew that I desperately needed to find work. Reluctantly, I returned to America to do so with the hope that I would soon return to continue my life with Jean Claude.

* * *

Quickly I was offered a job working in the abortion clinic of a well-known hospital in New York City. The year was 1970 and abortion had not long since been made legal in New York State. That part was easy. I knocked on a door and it opened. However I could no longer tolerate what surrounded the offer. The noise, the dirt, the sheer size of New York, and the magnitude of its buildings repelled me. I felt dwarfed by them and battered by the racket. I rejected the job offer. I would go into the countryside, I thought. It would be cleaner and quieter there. So I found work as a school social worker in Ellenville, a small village in upstate New York. I started in January. Snow covered everything. I rented the upstairs apartment of a little house whose back windows overlooked a stream cutting its way through the snow.

But I missed Jean Claude, and he wanted to join me. He had never been to America. In preparation for his arrival, I found a job for him. The brother of my friend and past supervisor when I worked for the child welfare department while living in Woodstock, New York, was close to the household of the composer Igor Stravinsky. He knew that they were looking for a cook in their New York City residence. I knew that Jean Claude was a great one. I sent him my first paycheck to buy a plane ticket. He arrived and interviewed for the job. He did not get it. After two weeks of unsuccessfully looking for work in New York, Jean Claude returned to Paris.

When spring arrived in Ellenville and the snow melted, my beautiful stream was full of discarded, plastic bottles and bags. I cried. When the school term ended, I handed in my resignation and returned to Paris with my newly earned American money. Jean Claude was waiting for me.

While I had been away, he had given up his flat in Athens for lack of funds. We wanted to live in Greece, but Hydra was too expensive. However we learned that the island of Symi in the Dodecanese, not far from the Turkish border and a twelve-hour ferry trip from Athens, would not be. We had heard that Symi, like Hydra, was a beautiful, light-filled island. Also like Hydra, it had no roads and no cars, along with many more empty houses. It had been a wealthy sponge diving center until synthetic sponges transformed its commerce.

Symi was sparsely populated with residents consisting mostly of black-clad women with children, waiting for checks sent by their husbands who had gone abroad to find work. We eventually found a large and splendid house with painted ceilings, marble floors and tall French doors opening onto balconies that faced the sea. In summer the house was so hot that we could see heat waves rising from the pavement below. In winter, we froze. The one small kerosene stove that we kept in the bedroom was no help, once we left the bed. So we lingered there as long as we could. Hunger and the need for water, which had to be drawn from a deep well in the kitchen below, were the only things that kept us moving during that freezing winter.

In summer, many guests came to visit from Paris. They were either artists, mistresses of artists, or benefactors of artists. One of these guests, an elderly film director who constantly wore a scarf tied around her aging neck as if to hide sagging flesh, once asked me if my mother knew where I was. Her tone was nasty, but it jolted me into realizing that I was with a man fourteen years older than me, a man whom she might have wanted for herself. She had attacked my innocence, and for the first time, I became aware of feeling vulnerable. I put her question out of my mind then, but it has always remained with me. How could I have been so out of touch with the reality of my situation?

In 1973, after living on this island for a year and a half, money ran out again. I knew that this time, I could not return to America. I had lived for too long abroad. I would not be able to acclimate to an American lifestyle, where women were throwing off their bras, garbage littered the streets of New York, and loud disco music accompanied the use of heavy drugs. Jean Claude said that I would love England because he did. I had heard that the country was looking for American-trained social workers. I left Symi with 196 English pounds in my pocket after having gone to Rhodes to exchange what remained of my Greek money. I somehow knew that Customs required 200 pounds for entry into England. I was fearful that I would be turned away, but I felt that I had no other option. As I waved to Jean Claude from the ferry that was to take me from Symi to Rhodes to Athens and onto England, I thought repeatedly that I should not have left the island.

Several days later, having arrived in England without incident, I learned that mine had been the last flight out of Athens. There had been a military coup that forced the airports to close. I could not have been sent back by the authorities for insufficient funds even if they had wanted to.

I did like England. Jean Claude was right about that. And after many months, I did find work there. After four more years, I found a psychoanalyst with whom I discovered the meaning of the words "womanizing" and "alcoholism." I could no longer escape the fact that in my being lost, I had become the victim of these behaviors.

I believe that if it had not been for financial problems, I would have remained in Greece. The need for money, and the means of getting it, put some structure back into my life. It saved me from the endless wandering, the interminable hope that Jean Claude would want to change his life for me. My soul, in its homelessness, had been without roots. It was in danger of being destroyed. Somehow I knew these things without putting words to them.

So, I left the home that we had so lovingly made on Symi just as I had left my ex-husband. I threw a second dead fish back into the sea. I was, if not consciously moving on, moving elsewhere. This time, I landed on an analyst's couch in Little Venice, a section of London near Regent's Canal. I was paying for someone to recognize me. She did.

CHAPTER TWO:

THE JOURNEY

I shall start the tale of my search at its beginning. My father died of heart failure in 1945 when I was four years old. We lived in an almost rural section of northern New Jersey, west of the Hudson River, about an hour-and-a-half's drive away from New York City, if you were travelling in the heavy lumbering cars of those days. We lived on a small and quiet street with no sidewalks and few passing cars. By the time I was six, I would cross the road in front of our house to go into the woods. To the left of them was a house set back from the road. I imagined it to be a huge mansion, but I could not see it as it was hidden by its lush grounds. There was always, riddling the silence on a summer's day, the sound of a bird cooing. A pigeon, my mother said dismissively; but I, now grown-up, think it was a pair of doves.

At the entrance to the woods, was a leafy lane just wide enough for a single car. I had never seen a car go in there but tire tracks were imbedded in the soft earth. A little way back in the woods was a clearing. I followed the tracks while dragging an old blanket behind me so that I could lie down in the field's tall grasses. My brother was somewhere in the woods, usually down at the lake fishing in his kayak or laying traps for beavers. Sometimes I could hear him shout to one of the friends who would accompany him; but I was always alone.

I lay there looking up at the clouds searching for an image of my father's face. When I found it, I would gaze at him intently until the cloud formation moved onto something else. When there was a break in the clouds and the sun streamed through them, I would see him again. This time he was poised in the air like a trapeze artist, cavorting from one shining ray to another, escorted by an entourage of plump cherubim. Satisfied that I had been with him, I would gather my blanket and return home to my mother.

The template for "search" must have begun there: the silence, the emptiness in my stomach, the yearning that I would come to name as loneliness; and the fear that as I lay there in the tall grasses some snake would come out to bite me. All of those feelings became embedded deeply within me, waiting for a trigger incident to set them off again and again and again.

Because apart from these instances of lying on the floor of the woods looking for my father's face above me, I was unaware of missing anything, even him. But I suppose I developed a sense of longing that silently grew within me, becoming a part of me. I longed for something, someone who could make me feel right again, light-hearted, adorable, and loved. No words were ever put to these feelings, so I was forced to live them and relive them, these feelings that were given no name.

Years passed; my mother remarried. We moved from the house that my father had built for us into a pink ranch house that my stepfather had built for us, set in a suburban landscape far away from any woods. There were now three stepchildren, all older than my brother and me, a new baby, my half-sister, and another death in the family. My stepfather, who owned a small business, came home from his store at noon one day when I was fourteen years old and suddenly died of a heart attack. I searched no more. I knew that I would never have what I was wanting, a Dad.

We stayed on in the suburbs. My mother committed herself to looking after these grown children who could hardly take care of themselves. Their mother had died only two years before my mother married their father.

Their housekeeper, whom they had had for many years, was told to leave as soon as my mother arrived. They had no extended family that they had any attachment to, nor many friends, nor an ally in their own father. He was abrupt with them and seemed to want to pay attention only to me and to the baby. They were stunned, frightened, immobilized and damaged.

After his death, the elder of my two stepsisters, who by then was twenty-one years old, teased me endlessly. I was too dramatic when I played the piano; my singing only sounded good if I were surrounded by mountains as I had been in summer camp where I had the lead roles in the musicals; my friends were snobs and spoiled brats and on and on she went, always with a smile on her face and a ready laugh that made it difficult to think that her intentions were to malign me. My mother either did not notice or ignored the behavior in service of keeping the peace.

The other stepsister was eighteen years old by this time and the closest in age to me at fifteen. She and I shared a bedroom, but she hardly spoke to me or left our room, driving me out of it. She frightened easily. When her father was alive, he often took the entire family to his favorite restaurant on a Sunday, after which she predictably would vomit up her meal. She did have one friend who lived across the street, but she took no interest in school or its activities. The year after she graduated high school, she was married off by my mother, and shortly after that she became agoraphobic.

I was expected to help my mother look after her stepchildren and my baby sister. I did my best, but the empty feeling was back again. I wanted my mother, and I wanted things to be the way they were before my stepfather and his family came along, just the three of us living in the brick house across the road from the woods.

Although my brother and I never discussed the stepfamily, his grades at his new school were terrible. His new peers could neither hunt nor trap, two activities that my brother excelled at, and he was not good at their team sports. He bought himself a BB gun and shot at birds from the window of the bedroom that he shared with his decade-older stepbrother. I was put on patrol duty to see that my brother did not harm himself or anyone else. That was fine with me. As long as I could be near him, I didn't care what I was doing.

By then he had become what our family called incorrigible. He had failing grades, he was angry, he refused to do anything that would make him be like the others. He was sent away to boarding school when I was in the eighth grade and he was in his junior year of high school. Amongst this new family my mother acquired, I again felt alone.

My outlet was school. When we moved to the ranch house when I was twelve, I became suddenly popular. Teachers loved me. I worked hard to catch up with the others in this more sophisticated environment. Both girls and boys liked me. I had many friends. But by the time I reached my junior year in high school, I decided that I didn't want my friends anymore. I had no reason for this change of heart. It was as if some gray vapor had descended over me and separated me from everyone else. I brought books of my own choosing to school and hid them behind the textbooks so that I could read secretly. Then I would go home to teach myself the lesson I should have learned instead of reading Sartre and Camus.

I went away to college to study English literature at Boston University. Finally, I could leave home and do as I wished. My high school boyfriend was attending Harvard, and I assumed that we would continue our relationship. When, in my sophomore year, he told me that he had another girlfriend, I again changed. I became more reclusive than I had ever been but I did not attribute it to what had happened. I felt that I needed to hide myself, to become ugly. When I was a child, people had always said that I was going to be a beauty, that I looked like a pretty Irish girl, or that I looked like the girl on the Vermont Maple Syrup bottle, wholesome, a natural beauty. When I was in high school, I had been voted second best-looking brunette. But I no longer wanted people to say that I was pretty. I didn't want people to notice me at all. I only wanted to study until I couldn't see the print on the page anymore. Except for the odd fling with a boy from MIT or Harvard, I kept even more to myself.

Toward the end of my sophomore year, I met a fellow, a college drop-out, six years older than me who had his own apartment on nearby Symphony Road. I took to going around to his place to study and then I took to sharing his amphetamines. I can still smell the plastic capsules that we broke open in order to get an adrenalin rush from their cotton-soaked interiors. He taught me how to clean his toilet and how to boil an egg. I thought this was domestic bliss. He was a poet who was teaching himself to play the bass. With Charlie Parker playing in the background, I read and wrote papers, devouring the academic part of college.

After a year of this, I became ill with a severe case of mononucleosis. Again, I felt nothing, physical or otherwise. But my mother grew concerned. Her worries led her to discover my lifestyle. Horrified, she consulted my aunt who insisted on taking us all to a psychiatrist for advice. After two sessions, he told them to get me out of Boston. I resisted; but by then I had not the strength to go on fighting my mother. I left the poet and that same summer, began a relationship with the man who, a year later would become my first husband. We courted while I completed my last year of college in New York at The Columbia University School of General Studies. In August of 1963, I graduated with a degree in liberal arts from Boston University, married him, and moved upstate to the rural and very artsy community of Woodstock, all within the same week.

No more amphetamines. No more battles with my mother. Something else took their place. It was the Sixties, a few years before the music festival that was to become a part of Woodstock's folklore and the nation's. Bob Dylan occasionally sang in the local café, and there were always rumors that Joan Baez had come to visit him.

We were there because my husband had found a job teaching English at the local public high school. Among his many talents was that of knowing where to be at the right time and in what place. He thus steered us from state to state and continent to continent throughout the five years that we were married. I followed him willingly, this Harvard philosophy major who wrote short stories, the first of which was published in the *Saturday Evening Post* when he was twenty-one.

My first husband emitted such a strong sense of potential that it even seemed to have a smell. He was invigorating, possessing the certainty that anything could happen and it would always be good. Life felt limitless. Every door that we approached opened as though automatically. We went well together. We had good health, good looks, good manners. He was funny. I was sweet again. We made a fine couple.

Job opportunities were few in Woodstock, but I managed to find a job at the local social service department in the area of child welfare. Checking up on foster homes, I loved the freedom of driving my red VW convertible over empty mountain roads to arrive at remote houses overflowing with foster children. When I asked how things were going, the reply was always "Fine." It seemed so to me, too, because I had neither the skill nor the training to help children to know what they might be feeling. Similarly, I didn't have the sense to look beneath the surface of what I was seeing. But I liked my supervisor. We talked a lot about problems, our own as well as our clients, though without finding any solutions.

Then my husband found an agent at the William Morris Agency who got him into writing for television. We moved to New York City where the programs were being made. He began writing comedy for the Merv Griffin game show and making money. I went to graduate school for social work at New York University.

It was while feeling purposeless that I found myself in graduate school for social work on full scholarship after my husband and I left Woodstock in

1965. I thought that being a social worker was handing out charity baskets to the poor. I even had a relative who was a social worker. An administrator for a charity organization, she was a nice, smart, quiet woman. I could see myself being like her. She sometimes spoke of speeches that she had to give, or grant proposals that she had to write. I could do that, I thought.

But somehow I found myself in the stream for learning to do clinical work. I had not paid attention to the fact that there were different categories of social work. I was simply happy that I had a place to be everyday while my husband worked writing comedy. Now I too had a career path. But I was shocked out of my complacency as I came to have firsthand experience in the field. I was being trained to work with people with severe mental illness. For light relief, there were marital problems. It made little difference whether or not I was dealing with one spouse screaming at the other or a schizophrenic adolescent whimpering in a corner of his family circle. High emotions were thrown into my once empty basket and I was expected to sort them out. It was rather like being handed a full bedpan without anywhere to dump it.

While I was doing my training, my husband would joke that he was putting the garbage into the world and I was taking it out. True. But where to put it? In me as it turned out. I had to process it—or not. If I was able to make sense of these emotions, I was doing a good job. If they stayed with me and made me lose my already precarious balance, I was not succeeding. I was the strainer that purified the experience for the patient, and returned it to him or her in a form that was more manageable. It took me years to learn how this approach worked; and to believe that this could cure. It can. It does.

Our search for meaning intensified as we straddled the two worlds of being moneyed intellectuals and closet hippies. When we were not out clubbing with comedians, we were discussing Timothy Leary and higher levels of consciousness. We experimented with marijuana and LSD. I listened to the Beatles. Over and over I played their haunting song, "Yesterday."

And suddenly, the sense of longing was back along with the loneliness, the emptiness.

We extended our search. After I finished graduate school and my husband was certain that he could work from abroad, we travelled to London to learn to meditate with disciples of the Beatles' Maharishi. Surely we would find enlightenment there. But it didn't feel as if we had.

We went on to the Greek island of Hydra to befriend the Canadian singer and songwriter Leonard Cohen. Leonard sang about loneliness. Perhaps he would have discovered a way to dispel it.

We travelled to Hydra in November of 1967 and ended by staying until the end of the following spring, living amongst a motley group of exiled artists and writers. Our story ends there. My husband's search led him to spend a weekend with another woman and when he confessed this to me the day of his return, I knew that our marriage had failed. It was over, he and I. I felt certain of that. We parted ways.

I was to live and to work in Europe for the next twenty years, fifteen of them in England, the bulk of them spent lying on my analyst's couch in London. There, I found what I had been searching for.

* * *

I did not enter the analytic world until the mid-seventies when I was working in England for a non-profit organization that offered psychotherapy free of charge to anyone who asked for it. There I found myself surrounded by colleagues who were being analyzed while training to be analysts. Words like projection and archetypes and good breast/bad breast were becoming part of another new language for me. I needed to know what they really meant. I read Carl Jung and Melanie Klein and discussed the theories of the British School of Object Relations with staff at meetings, at lunch, at tea breaks. We discussed cases and theory endlessly; but I also wanted to know what it was like to lie on a couch in receipt of all of this.

I needed guidance in my field. I recognized that I was out of my depth. I needed guidance in my life. I found myself morphing into an English bluestocking. Why had I ended up in England after a divorce, a five-year-long relationship with a French painter, an empty bank account because I had been supporting us both, and an inability to readjust to an American way of life? These were questions that kept occurring to me and I had no answers. I was doggie paddling my way through unknown waters barely keeping my head up high enough to breathe. In fact, a lot of the time I was hyperventilating.

Why was I where I was and how did I get there? I looked at the wreck my life had become and held onto my job for dear life. It was mother's milk to me; and a new world was opening, an inner world that had been sealed off. This was true nourishment. I learned to thrive on it. It saved my life.

So I entered a new universe, the inner world. It eclipsed the old one, the outer world. And it was like that for a very, very long time. I was in a nine-year analysis in England. It took place for the most part three times a week, but it also went up to four times and towards the end, slid down to two. It seemed like one year. Time disappears when one is in analysis. The outer world loses its landmarks like times and years and events. We note them; but we rush back to that inner world where our energy lies because it is there where we learn to make sense of the outer world. Once committed to this process, it is like having a seductive and secret lover who beckons to his other to come home after a hard day's work. "Come," he says, "We will figure this out." My analyst had become the most important, the most positive presence in my life.

Once or twice I railed against her. "Nothing is happening," I screeched, "All of this navel gazing means nothing." Growth comes in stages, she would say to me, her patient voice keeping its soft, calm pitch. It was always enough to soothe me into another few years.

But I was changing. Just as one cannot feel one's feet growing until the old pair of shoes no longer fits and causes pain, so does the process of analysis develop so slowly that one does not realize its growth until the old behavior does not work anymore. It no longer engrosses us. We scramble to find another way. This in itself is a difficult and sometimes painful process. But when we do arrive in a new place, we tire of what we have known and like an old toy it is dropped in a corner of the room. At times, it is picked up again, but quickly dismissed as boring, or stupid, as in "What am I doing this for?" One moves away from it until it disappears altogether. One moves on.

I remember that in that first session with my analyst, I said that I did not want to change, that I only wanted to understand more about my life as it was. My analyst wisely did not reply to this. She sensed my fear. And she knew that it was emotionally appropriate for me to be afraid. The process, as I condense it here, sounds easy. It is not. It is painful to re-experience the past that was not allowed to be felt at the time. It is anxiety-producing to find one's self exposed, without that old comfortable T-shirt, soiled and riddled with holes to fling on when one can find nothing else comforting to wear. She knew about the unconscious. I obviously did not. Could I have put a word or image to what I was experiencing below the conscious level that was making me feel uncomfortable, I would not have needed my analyst. That is the point.

Sometimes behavior becomes so much a part of ourselves that we think it is normal, if we think about it at all. We accept how we feel as a way of life. It is the only way of feeling that we know, so how could we think of it as odd, or wrong? How can we know that certain behaviors are destructive if we have nothing to measure them by? We are still eating and working and socializing. We are still raising children, belonging to the PTA, going out with the girls for coffee, so what is wrong?

The answer? Everything else. Work does not feel right. It is boring or dull. Somehow life has not measured up to what we wanted it to be, but nothing is perfect, we say, and we shrug the feeling off. And then the big wipe-out happens. We find it hard to function. Our tempers flare over little things. We want to sleep a lot, or we've been caught having an affair, or we're drinking too much, or one of our children gets himself into trouble, or there never seems to be enough money because we are getting and spending heedlessly. When such events occur, we are lucky because only then might we drag ourselves to safety in our need for relief, or for answers. Then there is hope for more than just survival. There is hope for truly living.

My story is one such story. I became, after eight more years of being psychoanalyzed in this country (but this time only once a week) a psychoanalyst as well. I had reached the top of the mountain and could look down on a landscape that was not only familiar to me, but one that I could understand. And I could give that understanding to others. That emotion would have seemed heady, had it not felt so natural and so real.

What became surreal was my past life. How could I have done the things I did? Things that killed my spirit and some that nearly killed my soul. Not to mention my body. And the whole time that all this was occurring I thought I was doing nothing wrong.

* * *

An analyst's life is interwoven with her work, with her patients. The two together form a third element that transforms both of them. It is, as Jung said, a form of alchemy. One cannot predict the results of the journey at the start. Freud used the analogy of a train journey. However, that implies that we know our destination and are headed for it. All of that may be true, but the journey is more like that of the Orient Express. The train stops along the way at places where one can get off, explore and return or not.

Sometimes the exploration leads to choosing a destination that we had not anticipated. Sometimes it leads to stopping and staying where we have disembarked. Perhaps we have had enough of therapy, or we want to proceed with life from where we are as a result of the treatment so far. Life looks good to us and full of potential and so we stop, even though we could have used a bit more help in reaching our potential. Or, sometimes therapy stops because of a total derailment of the relationship between patient and analyst. But this rarely happens if the two elements in the test tube, patient and analyst, are committed both to each other and to the work.

I have been intrigued by this underlying psychoanalytic process; that is, the dance between patient and analyst. I like to think of it as the unconscious part of the treatment. If we cannot always understand this process, we must at least acknowledge its importance. It is the analysts' job to understand ourselves. That is a given, one of the requirements of the profession. It is, of course, also our job to understand our patient. Each has their own history. It is the intertwining of the two that drives treatment.

The particular interactions that occur between uniquely individual patient and uniquely individual analyst have over the years impressed me. I will say more about it later, this behind-the-scenes effect of analysis. The way patient and therapist work together is fed by each of the lives and histories they have lived prior to the patient coming through the door for the first time. Yes, theory matters, technique matters. But here are two people in a test tube squashed together for years having the unspoken parts of their lives, their inner worlds, their unconscious impinge on one another. The analyst must know his own psyche in order to understand that of his patient. He must know when to keep it separate from that of his patient's and when to use it as a tool to understand her or him.

This union is sheer poetry written by an unseen hand. It is fiction. It is memoir. It is the skeleton of analytic work.

CHAPTER THREE:

BROTHER

When my brother and I were young, we looked so much alike — the same thick black hair, light blue eyes and white skin—that we were often taken for fraternal twins, even though he is three years older than me. Our birth dates, however, are nearly identical. He was born on March 21 and I on March 23. Before I was born, my mother predicted that he was going to have a little sister as his birthday present that year. Ever since, he has treated me like his gift, a very precious gift to whom he has given unconditional love.

After our father died in the winter of 1946 at the age of thirty-two, he became not only brotherly toward me but also fatherly. He never hesitated to tell me to shut-up or go wash my dirty face, and I didn't wait to shoot back that I would not do so as my "doity" face was clean. He'd laugh and give in to me. His attitude was never a matter of wanting to control me for control's sake. It was more one of benign guidance that he seemed to offer diligently and effortlessly.

For him, the loss of our father when he was seven years old and I was only four, came abruptly and unexpectedly. My mother had been told by the doctor in New Jersey, where we lived, that she had to get my father to a warmer climate and so my parents rented an apartment in Florida for that purpose. Our family was not new to Florida. My father's parents wintered there in the chic, Art Deco hotels of Miami Beach. They always invited us to join them, and so in the winter of 1943, we did.

The war was on. I remember troops of soldiers practicing their maneuvers on the beach near the blanket where we camped. The soldiers called out to my father in an unfriendly manner. My mother, much later, told us that they were chiding him for being with his young family rather than in the Army with them, healthy-looking as he was. My father had tried to enlist, but had been rejected because of his bad heart. The rejection was a source of shame for him. After that humiliating episode he stayed away from that beach.

Unaware of the serious nature of our father's condition, my brother accepted the fact that he had to stay home this time with our Aunt Esther so that she could look after him, as he was in second grade and had to go to school. I was not yet old enough for kindergarten. I could go with the little party that included my parents and my father's mother, who would look after me while my mother cared for my father. My father's father had died a few months earlier at the age of fifty-two, throwing even more of a pall over our journey.

My father died in February of 1946 after we had been in Florida for six months. The night before, I had been allowed to sleep in the empty hospital bed with the oxygen tent suspended over it that had been set up for him in the airy living room of the Spanish-style building in which we were staying. That day, he must have taken a turn for the worse because he had to be admitted to the hospital. In the middle of the night my mother received the phone call saying that he had died.

I can still hear her shriek, as in my mind's eye I see her standing in the dim, yellow light of the front hallway furnished only with a big black rotary phone sitting on a small table. I knew that something had gone horribly wrong. I had never before heard my mother make such a noise. I was "along for the ride," so to speak, as children often are when they witness things that they can't make sense of. But somehow I knew that nothing had been enough to keep my father's heart pumping. Not even me, his constant companion in that living room that had become his sickroom that had become our playroom.

My brother had not been told how ill our father was. He learned of his death four days later when we pulled up to our red brick house with the huge maple tree in the front yard, now bare of leaves. Someone had been assigned to collect us from Penn Station in Newark where the sleeper cars landed. I don't remember who it was. I remember my mother dressing me in a white blouse and plaid pleated skirt while I stood on the seat of the train before we disembarked, and I remember that for most of the journey, I was allowed to walk up and down the aisles by myself talking to everybody, telling them my father was riding on the roof.

One nice couple befriended me and later sent a box of candy to my home. I also remember my mother, who was then thirty-one, and my grandmother sitting silent in those dark plush seats of the train, inert. Those gray faces, one so young and the other grown so quickly old sitting side by side, were my first sight of depression. They are positioned in my mind alongside the famous Edvard Munch painting of "The Scream."

Although my mother had somehow informed my aunt of the death, it was thought best to conceal it from my brother whose behavior, understandably, had been difficult enough in our long absence without this upsetting news. In fact, he was never told, but he knew as soon as he saw that our father did not get out of the car with us, that he was dead, and he burst into uncontrollable sobbing. Even if I did not know how to name the illness that had killed my father, I had seen his blue lips well before we went to Florida. I even have a memory of my father cutting his hand once on a can opener and I swear that the blood spurting out from that deep cut was blue. Having had rheumatic fever when he was a child had weakened his aortic valve beyond repair. This I learned much later. My parents had both lived in denial of that fact, keeping their eyes shut and their fingers crossed as if in an effort to ward off death.

I have many memories of those times before my father died, times when he was healthy enough to play with us and take us with him to work, of being held in his arms, while he sold paint and other building supplies to local customers. My father had had the foresight to store huge supplies of paint and turpentine before the war, which were now in great demand. His business, shared with his brother who manned the store in town, was thriving.

I also remember my brother fishing with him in Florida during the winter of 1943, me watching, or venturing into the ocean with his arms wrapped tightly around me, and mine, clasped around his neck. He taught me to color and to keep within the lines — in the process teaching me to respect boundaries, I realized many years later.

He also played with both of us together. I can see my brother's head and mine bent over a table as our father instructed us about something. What was it? Learning to play cards? I don't remember exactly which game, but it never mattered exactly what we did. What mattered was that he was teaching us how to be together without him. Teaching us how, when he was gone, to carry on as if he were there, still guiding us, still wanting us to love and respect one another, and, especially for me, to follow my brother who was older than I, who knew more than I, and who was a male.

After his death, when I was five years old and my brother eight, we behaved with each other as if he were still there, as if we were the three of us still, only with one physically absent. By being the three us together my father had taught us how to be the two of us without him. There was a space that neither one of us ever spoke of but which remained with us, moving with us, being with us. I can't even call it spirit because as a child I didn't know the meaning of that word. It felt more like a white cushion-like space, not a sad one but rather a comforting one that the two of us held between us.

Never a playful parent, my mother was very present when my father was alive, but she always seemed to be busy doing other things. It had been my father, my brother, and I in our own little world, a contented threesome. Then he died. Then my mother sank into depression. Then my brother and I were a twosome.

I remember most vividly those times when our mother was unavailable to us. I can still see my brother on school mornings standing barefoot at the kitchen stove and holding onto the handle of a saucepan in which he was warming milk for our hot chocolate. I would stand in the doorway, barefoot too, not knowing what next to do and so I would watch him, his black hair tousled and his white skin marked from the pillow on which he'd slept. When he filled our cups, I would move to his side. He would hand me my cup and together we would stand on the cold linoleum floor drinking our breakfast.

Then when he headed towards our shared bedroom, I would know it was time to brush my teeth, fling cold water on my face, and comb my hair with my fingers, as he did, my thick black hair so exactly like his. After that, I would go to dress, and he'd be waiting at the kitchen door on the side of the house, watching to see that all was clear of the children who sometimes taunted us. They taunted us because we were plump, we were half-orphaned, we were Jews new to living in their Christian neighborhood and because they could sense that we were vulnerable.

My parents had never been religious although Jewish holidays were quietly celebrated amongst the extended family. My paternal grandfather, who had become a house builder, was buying up land in our neighborhood for development as well as for homes for his four children. He was a businessman, a family man and an ambitious man who wanted to build an empire for his sons. It is unlikely that the religion of his soon-to-be neighbors ever crossed his mind.

My brother took me to school and collected me afterward. Sometimes he would have to hold my hand while we ran together from some mean skinny boys who threw stones at our backs as we fled. At night, in our shared bedroom, he would hear me pray, something that I learned to do at school where we recited the Lord's Prayer each day. No matter how quietly I whispered to God, asking Him for "A"s in school and making certain that God knew "A" stood for being the best and not for the worst as in the word "awful," my brother's voice would break the darkness like the crack of a whip. "I can hear you," he would say. I was afraid that he would call me a sissy baby, but he never did. I would continue to whisper my prayers while pretending to be asleep with the covers over my head.

My brother never said his prayers. After our father died, there were no prayers for him, no wonder, no Santa Claus, no God. There was nothing but our mother who stayed in bed half the day and went about in her nightclothes the other half. And there was me. In retrospect I believe that looking after me gave my brother something to do. It made him feel big and grown-up. And he wasn't afraid of me in the way that he was when he knew it was his turn to get up to bat, or to take a test at school. I was controllable, not like his father dying or his mother feeling so sad and afraid.

He was so smart, this plump, curly-haired boy in short pants with a warm smile. He always knew the answer to any question I asked him. "Where is Alaska?" I would ask out of the blue and he would know where and what it was. The same with Eskimos and igloos and how many words the Eskimos had for "snow." But he would not attend to his schoolwork. He wanted to be out of doors in the woods across the road or out on the town lake, or setting traps for muskrats in the nearby swamp. There lay his freedom and as much as I wanted to tag after him, I knew somehow that I should not. I knew this was his private world where he experienced the freedom to just be a boy.

By the time that I was nine and reaching fourth grade, five years after my father's death, my mother finally emerged from her depression and we were three again, but this time it was frequently two against one. My brother and I joined forces against my mother in defiance of her. I suppose we were punishing her for having bailed on us. Sometimes we would lock ourselves in the bathroom and figure out how we could stay there forever so as not to be with her. We could live on toothpaste and tap water or maybe climb out of the bathroom window and run away. There were other dramas, involving packed bags and dramatic doorstep conversations. But all of that was much later. In 1953, seven years after my father died, when I was in fifth grade, my mother began dating. She married my stepfather at the end of that year. Then everything changed.

Joe, eleven years older than my mother, was a widower of two years with three children in their mid to late teens. He seemed besotted with our mother's natural, good looks and spent every minute away from his work being with her. Her naivete, her innocence seemed to act as an added stimulant for his adoration of her that, at the same time, was somehow tinged with ridicule. I remember he teased her about having a shiny nose because she wore no make-up, confusing me about whether or not that was a good thing. He also didn't seem to like my brother being around, and told my mother he needed more discipline, which he promptly began issuing.

Because of my brother's suddenly failing grades despite his high IQ and his refusal to accept his stepfather as an authority figure, he was sent away to boarding school in the northwestern part of New Jersey. We had been living in West Orange for nearly two years by then, far away it seemed from any of our own relatives who were in Morristown. Escaping the "melded" family was the beginning of my brother's long climb back to take his place in the world. And that was the beginning of my slipping out of the world. Within a year or two of his departure, I began isolating myself from my friends, my family, and especially my mother. But I never left my brother, and he never abandoned me. When he came back from school during breaks, he would share with me reading lists for the subjects he was studying, his newly discovered love of jazz, his friends, among them two single-parent brothers who came from South America. We would talk about things like how to define Beauty.

As my brother and I grew older we inevitably grew away from each other. By 1961, he had married and started a family. I had married my first husband and then left the States for Europe where I remained for nearly twenty years. We corresponded on occasion, and I always visited my brother and his family while on visits to my mother, but those were also infrequent. It was there in England in 1980, when I was thirty-nine and well into my first psychoanalysis, that I suddenly realized how much a part of me he was.

Psychoanalysis has a way of making us conscious of the good as well as the bad. It brings an awareness to our lives that can make us feel so many disparate things—pain, anger, gratitude and eventually, sometimes, forgiveness. But none of this comes with intellectual understanding alone. The rest of it involves hanging on for dear life to a trusted analyst as the stories we tell her and the tears we shed form a mosaic somewhere deep within us.

We sometimes cannot see the new pattern that has formed until an unexpected catalyst occurs and then "Bango!" we are doing something new, something that we have yearned to do, something that we have talked about doing for years on the analyst's couch, something that we thought we would never be able to and here it is and we are doing what we have quietly dreamed about and hardly dared to imagine. And it happens seamlessly. The world, our world, is expanding and once we get over the fear of that expansion, we will be in a new place and it will feel like home. Psychoanalysis is mind expanding and therefore, life expanding. If psychoanalysis can boast of anything it is of cultivating awareness about the lives that have been given to us, and the lives we have lived, so that the future can be ours to choose.

And so it was, on the day my brother and his wife came to visit me in England while vacationing with some friends, that I learned, at age thirty-nine, how deep and unshakable was my love for him. They had taken me out to dinner in London, and when the evening ended my brother walked me to where my trusty Morris Minor was parked and we kissed and said good-bye.

It was while I was navigating the car around busy Piccadilly Circus, where roads from all over London seem to converge in madcap fashion that I burst into loud wracking sobs. I could hardly see the crowded roadway as tears flooded my face. I suppose I was driving every which way because I was stopped by the police. They asked me what I thought I was doing. Still unable to control my crying I replied, "My brother came to visit from the States. He's leaving. I can't bear it." In retrospect I can see that the intensity of that entire experience, along with others, fed my abrupt decision to return home.

My mother's words had indeed been prophetic, but in reverse. It was not I who was a gift to him, but he who was a gift to me. His sweetness of nature and generosity of self are boundless. I once had a wise-guy sort of boyfriend in the States who jealously called my brother, "Mr. Walk on Water." Some metaphors are indeed accurate.

CHAPTER FOUR:

MOTHER

My mother once made a significant confession to me regarding our relationship. Actually I count it as two confessions, one made directly after the other. It was while I was deeply involved in my first analysis in England, somewhere in the late 1970s. It was Christmas. I was thirty-five years old. I had returned to America for a ten-day visit, a rare event in those days. My mother was still living in the house in the suburbs where I had seen Joe, my fifty-two-year-old stepfather, die of a massive heart attack twenty-one years earlier. As I was kneeling on the floor to unpack my suitcase, she looked on from her seat on the sofa behind me and commented that I always carried bundles like a bag lady.

Jet-lagged and exhausted after a sleepless night on a crowded economy flight, I was rifling through my luggage to find the gift that I had brought for her. Her words made me stop for a moment. I could feel my back stiffen, but I suppressed myself from saying, "Burdens." I thought bitterly, "They are not bundles but burdens, and why don't you help me to carry them?" There was a silence. Light filtered in from the picture window behind her, showing a dull short street that ended in a cul-de-sac. The street was edged with brown houses set a little way back from the road as if kneeling on their haunches, the better to see into the neighbors' houses directly opposite. Back in the mid-1950s when my mother and stepfather built the pink-bricked ranch house for their newly melded family, it had seemed shiny and impressive, fringing as it did on the best neighborhood in West Orange, New Jersey. Now it seemed shamefully dated and dull, like an old woman wearing the party dress of her teens.

My mother spoke again, this time addressing my back. "Bevie," she said, "I have not been a good mother to you." My heart jerked. That statement was followed by, "And I am done feeling guilty about it."

It was my turn to be silent again. And silence was the state that I continued to be in until her death, ten years ago at the age of ninety-six. She died then, because she wanted to die. There was nothing wrong with her physically, but I learned after her death, that she had had Lewy Body Dementia. At its onset when I came to visit her one day, she told me that she had tried to kill herself by sitting at the kitchen table and holding her breath. I laughed, impatient with hearing anything that touched on the theme of her perpetual sadness, which began with my father's death and continued on throughout her life in various stages of remission and resurgence. Afterwards when I understood about this form of dementia, the same disease that had killed the actor Robin Williams in 2014, I felt badly for having been annoyed at her distress.

After Joe's death, when she was forty-one, I had grown accustomed to hearing her jokingly call herself "The Black Widow," a reference to the black widow spider who kills her mates once she is impregnated. My mother had a total of two husbands, ten years of marriage, and six children as the result. She was not about to try her luck in marriage again. When I would say, "Mom, don't call yourself the Black Widow. Those deaths were not your fault," she would look at me with set lips as if to say, "What do you know about death?"

I have often wondered if my mother's anger, begun in her childhood and never expressed, was further validated by these deaths. My maternal grandmother was a very busy woman, having arrived in this country at the age of sixteen, married at eighteen, and had two children following in quick succession by the time she was twenty. She did not speak English so she took lessons at the local "neighborhood house" down the street, her babies in her arms. At the same time, she was caring for newly arrived immigrants from Russia, to whom she was renting rooms on the third floor of her house. In addition, she was starting an antique business with my grandfather.

There is a photo taken during this period of a beautiful, somber-faced child, who is my mother, sitting with arms and legs crossed, wearing a dress crocheted by my grandmother and sporting a frivolous, huge satin bow in her dark hair. Her brother and younger sister are similarly attired with my uncle in sailor suit and Dutch Boy haircut looking every bit the family prince, which he was, and my aunt wearing the same crocheted dress, but smaller with an equally large bow in her light-colored hair and showing tightly closed, angry-looking fists. My Aunt Esther was openly angry and fought hard for what she later accomplished. My uncle, being my grandmother's only son, got the best of everything including the only steak at dinner and the college education, while the girls did not. My mother, who would never fight about anything, had always felt deprived and overlooked. I can imagine my busy grandmother telling my mother not to move out of the chair that she had assigned her, or else. When she finally did, by marrying my father and then my stepfather, she got her punishment.

Why did my mother want to die? Because she had had enough of us, her children, her family, her old age. She'd always had excellent health and when she began to lose her hearing, she was impatient at wearing hearing aids. When her eyesight grew worse, she refused to get stronger glasses. Aging to her was a personal affront that was hard to bear in her solitude, where she'd had enough of mourning for the life that she never had. I was sixty-nine years old when she died at age ninety-six. Her last gesture towards me was to take my hand in hers. That touch remains there, held in the palm of my hand as a treasured gift. My mother was never affectionate toward me, although she was with my brother calling him, "tottie," Yiddish, I suppose, for the word "boy." She loved him, and she loved boys. Girls, she would always say, were difficult.

And so I was by the time I reached my teens in the 1950s. Until then I had been her good child, her handmaiden, her caretaker, her companion, and her friend. I had been a part of her, carried inside of her as if I were another bodily organ. I had been fused with her. This symbiotic state was a creative solution to not having her at all.

After my own father's death, she turned away from us. My father's family, although they lived within short blocks of us, stayed away. My father's mother was in mourning for her husband and her son, who had died eight months after my paternal grandfather. My paternal grandfather had been the one person my mother admired in my father's family, and he had loved my mother in return. With him gone and my grandmother's increasing needs since the deaths of her son and husband, my mother kept her at a distance. She had never liked my father's family much anyway because she felt my father was too attached to them. My mother had wanted him for herself and waged her battle there, perhaps the only one she had ever fought in her life. I remember my parents fighting when I was very young. I recall one episode when my father locked my mother out of the house. She stood enraged on the front landing banging at the door, but the three of us, pushing against it from the inside, did not allow her in until my father said that we should.

After my father died, my mother took her anger to bed turning it into a depression that made her sleep a lot. She would be asleep when we left the house for school, my older brother getting me ready, dropping me off at the playground where I stayed on its edge watching the others at play. I was preoccupied with worry about her. I had no friends. I didn't know how to skip or jump rope the way the others did. Play seemed silly to me, and the others who did it, stupid. When my brother brought me home at lunchtime, my mother would be quietly padding about the kitchen, still in her nightgown, preparing a can of Campbell's tomato soup for us. Then she would return to her bed until we got home again at three, when she would emerge subdued, showered, silent, withdrawn. She would fix us dinner and eat with us, but it was as though she were enveloped in a shroud.

I thought about her all the day while at school, wanting to be with her in order to be sure that she was alright. I suppose I was afraid that she too would die and leave us. When I returned home from school, I never left her side. In the night, always at three a.m., I would walk my little fingers across the silent walls of the dark hallway connecting my bedroom with hers until I reached her bed to lie with her, back-to-back, feeling her warmth through the thin nylon membrane of her nightgown. In the morning, I would awaken to gaze into her sleeping face where I saw the tears from the night before, pooled still between the corner of her eyes and the bridge of her nose.

She was beautiful, my mother, with her dark curly hair, high cheek bones and aquiline nose. "Madonna della rosa", Mother of Sighs, I nicknamed her for my analyst thirty years later. It hurt less that way. I know now that she wanted to die when we were children. Depression was as close as she got to death in those days. It was a solution to not knowing what to do with us, her children, or how to live without him, my father.

I think the only thing that kept my mother from being terminally depressed was another battle that she fought, this one with my father's family over money.   My father had left no will. His business had to be divided and sold off, along with various properties that had been held in common. Although she thought that she had lost this bewildering, victimizing battle, in fact she won it, as it forced her to leave the house if only to go to the lawyer's office in town in order to settle the estate.

Over the next seven years, her depression gradually ebbed, at which point she met Joe. He was red-haired, small and wiry, and cracked jokes. He dressed in silky-looking double- breasted suits that he bought from his brother Babe's clothing store. My mother always told us that she married him because he made her laugh. By doing this, he seduced away the rest of her blues. And then he seduced her body. It was 1952. Joe owned his own store, a liquor and grocery in a neighborhood where there were a lot of alcoholics. He worked until ten pm six days a week, twelve-hour days, and my mother, after she had given us all supper, would sometimes keep him company while he entertained her by poking fun at his befuddled, unsuspecting customers.

She was lost to me again. She didn't need me, but this time because she was happy. They married quickly. I was sent off to summer camp the first year of their marriage, and I was happy, too. They came to visit my brother and me. Mother looked lovely in a pink maternity frock trimmed with white angora embroidered flowers, my half-sister now fully ensconced in her pregnant belly. She was thirty-nine years old to Joe's fifty. Eighteen months later he died of a sudden, massive heart attack.

He left her with my half-sister who was an eighteen-month old infant, the three stepchildren, who were a twenty year-old son still in college and two step-daughters in their mid to late teens, my brother who had escaped to boarding school by then, me, still her handmaiden but mildly protesting, and little else as far as I know. This time she turned to the neglected, helpless stepchildren instead of to depression. When my own father died, there was money enough from his growing business and real estate properties, so that his widow would never have to work. She decided to work for the stepchildren, to befriend them and make them better. Their own mother had died years before, they had been ignored by their hard-working father and my mother set out to make it up to them.

She fed them, paid for them, encouraged them, joked with them, spoiled them with their favorite chocolate cakes, left at all times on the corner of the dining room table for their nibbling comfort whenever they passed by. The sight of chocolate cake crumbs still has the power to repel me. The crumbs overflowed the dining room table onto the floor and were trekked everywhere.

She also cleaned up after her stepchildren, endlessly emptying their overflowing ashtrays. She enlisted me to do the same. I followed after her, eager to help her because she would often complain to me about them, and I could now, and yet again, be her confidant. I had a position. I had a place still inside of her, and one outside as well as helping her with the endless household chores that the stepsisters relentlessly inflicted on us, treating us as if we were the housekeeper they had lost when my mother married their father.

I cannot talk more about them as it still causes me pain to know that my mother chose them over me. And she did so, I believe, as a way of avoiding a return to her depression. After my own father died, she had surrendered herself to its soft embrace. Gradually that depression receded, and then she discovered laughter with Joe. When he died, the laughter died too.

So it was I who was there alone when my stepfather died in his turquoise armchair in our living room. I was fourteen years old and it was 1955. The broken vessels, the stepchildren, were not there, but I was, with my new baby half-sister, whom I had been taking care of in my arms. Minutes before, I had been frantically ordered by my mother to hold my sister and to watch out for Joe's return home. Joe was very ill, she told me. He had had to shut his liquor store and go to the doctor, who had written a prescription for him which was due to arrive while she, my mother, had to run an errand.

My seventeen-year-old brother had been to a spring prom the night before, and his rented tuxedo had to be returned that day or there would be another day's charge. She had to deliver it to the dry cleaner's, she said, and would be back soon. None of this, except her sense of panic, penetrated me at the time. She was out the front door before I could ask any questions.

I have been trying ever since to understand her actions, although I never felt brave enough to ask her directly or to ever refer to that death scene. How could she leave me alone holding the baby at this time of crisis? How could she desert Joe, her beloved husband who was so ill, for a tuxedo? I think now that she simply did not know what to do. She was gripped by panic. She had no thought for me or my infant sister. She needed to escape the whole mess. She was trying to ground herself by grasping onto the mundane errand of returning a $14.95 rented tuxedo. I was left to figure out the rest.

I was fourteen years old. I could not figure out what was happening. My stepfather died while I watched him die, a terrified few feet away and with my baby sister asleep in my arms. The truth is that this death scene of 1955 has not been one that has ever been excavated in my seventeen years of analysis. Nor is it a secret, although it feels like one, perhaps only because when I have mentioned it to other people, with the exception of my sister, I have had no feedback. I could not stop my stepfather's death simply because I did not know what to do.

I had watched as he hurled himself through the heavy aluminum screen door a few minutes after my mother left, stumbling sideways into a chair. I had been standing on the back porch with its big picture window framing the scene in front of me. I had heard him fighting death, trying to scare it off with the funny-sounding rattles that were coming from his throat. I hear them still. Fascinated, driven by a sense that I had to do something, I had slowly walked from the porch into the kitchen where I listened through the open door to the dining room and watched from the mirror opposite, which was hanging over the elaborate oak buffet.

A few more slow seconds and I had moved into the dining room, watching him from an angle. His head was thrown back in an effort to gasp for air. The noise had become more guttural and intense and I slowly realized that it was being interrupted by screaming. It was my mother as she ran through that same heavy remorseless door, which had torn off one of her shoes, leaving it lying sideways on the threshold.

Following her was a young man who turned out to be the drugstore delivery boy. She tore the paper bag from his hand, opened the medicine bottle, and pushed her fingers all the way back into Joe's throat, the pill that was to save his life. It was too late. She had quickly realized that he was dead, grabbed my sister from me where I was by now leaning against the wall trying to make myself as small as possible, and ran screaming into their bedroom slamming the door behind her. I had stood there for a long time, it seemed, while the corpse in front of me seemed to stiffen in the chair. The delivery boy took over, got things moving by calling the police. I don't even know the boy's name.

The situation remains a fossil somewhere in the center of my Self. I can move it around a little. I rearrange it like furniture trying to find the best feng shui position. I play with it as I used to play with my paper dolls, alone, trying to make the best use of the clothes that I had cut out for them. My mother and I never discussed what had happened. Why would we? I was a part of her and she was part of me. For her, it would have been like talking to herself, which she did silently and often. Only I could never hear her.

As the years passed, my mother stayed at home more and found a routine in her housekeeping that became predictable. She would arise from her bed after the others had long gone to work or to school and sit at the kitchen table in her nightdress and scuffed slippers and sip coffee made from a two-cup aluminum percolator, staring out the kitchen window while munching on dry rye toast smeared with pot cheese.

She would think about what to make for dinner and end up by serving several different meals at once in order to still please the stepchildren. I was never asked. I would not anyway have known what to tell her because my wants and needs were such a blur by then. Seated at the kitchen table eating with the others, I would try not to get caught reading a book hidden in the napkin in my lap while they were all telling my mother about their boring (to me) day. But I always did get found out, and grudgingly would put the book behind me until I could escape to it after I had done the dishes.

After I left home to go to college in 1959, four years after Joe's death, my mother had finally got round to planting a lone rosebush in the backyard, something which she had been talking about wanting to do ever since she had moved into that house. I had just returned for summer vacation that first year and kissed her hello when she took my hand to pull me out of doors to see the single rose that it had produced. There was the scraggy bush set in the middle of an otherwise barren backyard where the grass had been scalded by the sun, rimmed by the neighbors' carefully trimmed hedges. I had been eager to tell her about the long, shared ride home from Boston, my exam grades, my summer school plans. She was so proud to have produced this pink, scentless, suburban rose that my excitement was extinguished compared to hers. It was she who had achieved something. What I had achieved no longer seemed worth even talking about.

My mother was a nice person to everyone else, but she was not nice to me. That was because she treated me as she mostly treated herself, contemptuously, critically, ignoring the good and scolding herself for the bad. She saw in herself, and by extension in me, what was missing rather than what was fully there. She did this because she assumed that I was exactly like her. That I *was* her. She gave me no space of my own to grow into because she made the mistake of believing that I was not separate from her. I needed no space, she believed. I needed nothing beyond that which she thought I should have, as she would have had it for herself had not death intervened.

I don't think that my mother ever did know who I really was because I was either being carried contentedly around inside her or, as I grew older and too big to fit into that space, I was fighting with her over the mistakes she was making. I had become angry, too, about her alignment with Joe's family. I knew that she needed them, but they were in the way.

Unmovable and triumphant over me, or so it seemed, this artificially arranged family system finally came apart at the very end. The stepsister who became agoraphobic never left her house for forty-five years until the day the ambulance men came to take her away to be hospitalized for her many neglected illnesses. She died there soon after, and my mother finally stopped sending her a birthday check every year, her only contact with her over those many years, and mine, none at all. The other sister, who had become my mother's companion after I left home, eventually became ill and cantankerous. My mother had no patience for it. They, too, drifted apart.

But long before all of that happened, my mother and I had given up on each other in despair. We turned away to look elsewhere for connectedness—she to her baby and the stepchildren, and I, to boys and later men. As years passed, it became more and more obvious that we had each found the wrong kind of connectedness.

It was my first analyst, whom I saw when I was thirty-five years old, who used the term symbiotic to describe our relationship. It made me think of monkeys nestled together or lichen on tree stumps. My second analyst gave the relationship no label but stated quite plainly that my mother obviously did not like me. I remember feeling hurt, and I told him that that wasn't so, but he insisted. "Your mother never liked you," he said. "She does not like you now." He was right, but he left me to fill in the blanks. My mother didn't like me because she didn't like herself, and I was she. It was like that philosophical puzzle where one element is subsumed in another. Perhaps it was that she didn't like me from the beginning and so she made me a part of herself so that she would not neglect me entirely. I am grateful for even that.

Yet and still, to make matters more complicated, I do believe that she loved me, or at the least, finally came to respect me. She was an intelligent woman whose intelligence was carefully hidden away so that she could rely on being helped by being a helpless female in those days of 1950s femininity. I feel that she never really knew me. But perhaps that is the only way that some people can ever love anyone else: that is, by not really knowing them.

I loved her. And I still do, even though she has been dead for ten years and maybe because I have no need of her now. She was a good woman with good intentions and many fears that she would not ever try to overcome. After the deaths of her two husbands, it seemed that my mother had no goal in life beyond trying to endure it in the most comfortable way possible. After a time, many things became an effort to her. Unapologetically, she stopped cooking, wearing lipstick, buying anything new for herself. She needed and wanted a companion, but made no effort to find a suitable one. She did not need another child, a dependent or a daughter who separated from her.

She gave me my sense of values and my sense of beauty. In her quiet and mysterious way, she had a deep love of the natural world. It was there, and not in organized religion, that her spirituality found its place. It was she who sent me into the woods, who left me to play barefoot in the muddy road at the side of our house, who let me eat watermelon outdoors so that the juice could drip freely down the front of my warm summer body, while spitting the seeds back into the earth with delight. She drew pleasure from the sight of a pink flush on the cheek of a child returned home from play. She brought to my attention a brilliant sunset, a view. As a child I had felt a momentary irritation at these interruptions into my reveries. It was only much later that I would look and look again.

CHAPTER FIVE:

ON KINDNESS

Like a beautiful, silent cat entering a room without making a fuss, so did kindness enter my life. And because I had never given much thought to the whole concept of kindness, I ignored the fact that I was a recipient of it. So many other things were happening for me all at once when I was thirty-three, that I grew blind to details. That is what occurs when one jumps into the water alone, before knowing how deep it is, or how cold, or murky. Kindness is the reaching out of an arm belonging to a stranger in an attempt to prevent death by drowning.

So it was in 1973, when I arrived in England from the island of Symi, where I left Jean Claude behind in order to go in search of filling the coffers again. I had not wished for kindness. I had not known that I would need it or even want it, but it arrived as a gift to me from somewhere. Since then, I have randomly stumbled over it and caught myself feeling gratitude for its presence, and I have been especially thankful to the British people, who typically give it so willingly to one another and who extended it to me at this moment in my life. Ask for directions in busy London and if you have the look of a person who cannot understand English, someone will likely take you by the arm and lead to where you want to go. Sometimes, you don't even need to look uncomprehending. Was it the last war that had done this to them? Had that disastrous event created their deep sense of empathy for the helpless? For that, surely, was I.

After my money ran out for the second time when I was living in Greece—the money that I had earned during my brief interlude back in America in 1971—I eventually went to England to find employment. I had heard that they needed American-trained social workers there. They had recently implemented a robust social service system and wanted people who were knowledgeable about psychological matters. After living in Europe for six years, I knew that I could not readjust to life in America. It had been hard enough to do when I had worked in Ellenville, in that awful winter two years earlier. Now it seemed impossible.

I was thirty-three years old. I had no friends or even acquaintances living in England with the exception of one couple, also in their thirties, whom I had met several months earlier on the island of Symi. They had been passing through Greece on their way to England so that the woman, Dorothy, could give birth to their child. They, like me, had no money, and were going to England because she could give birth free of charge there. They were biding their time until that event drew nearer.

Dorothy was a petite Australian proudly sporting a pert rounded belly, and Glenn, her Canadian partner, was handsome, tall, and lean. Both were gentle and soft-spoken and had been long-time friends, travelling companions and lovers. When I told them that I was thinking of heading to England to find work, Dorothy, who had taken a liking to me, began immediately planning my future as if it were her own. "Do come to England," she urged. We'll help you find what you need there." Before embarking on their journey, she gave me an address in England where they could be reached.

I put it aside, but over the following weeks, I found myself not only including Dorothy and Glen in my plans to leave the island but also regarding them as my anchor. I would go to them, I thought, and the rest would follow.

I wrote them at the address they'd left with me and told them my date of arrival. They immediately replied that they had contacted a friend of theirs who lived in London who would meet me at the airport, bring me to her home for an overnight stay, and the next day drive me down to a village called Tunbridge Wells where Dorothy and Glen were living.

* * *

A few weeks later, when I arrived alone at Heathrow Airport at two in the morning, I was greeted by a woman whom I'd never met. The airport was silent and deserted at that early hour. The woman who looked to be in her thirties, was business-like, cordial but distant as anyone would likely be when offering that kind of early morning hospitality to a total stranger.

I was trembling. I attributed my fear to the long ride up the escalator from baggage claim, but in retrospect, I know it to have been another kind of fright. It was as if except for the few workers on duty, this woman and I were the only people in the quiet, near empty airport. When we spoke, which was not often, our voices echoed off the walls, and my uncertain footsteps clicked loudly on the concrete floor. For a year and a half, confined to the landscape of a small, barren Greek island, I had seen no escalators, no elevators, not even any cars. On Symi, nothing seemed to move unless sheer muscle power was applied.

After the perennial warmth of Greece, I felt cold on this chill November early morning. I felt alone, foreign and small, dwarfed by the size of the building and unaccustomed to its modern, minimalist look. I seemed an alien to myself, and of course in this country, I was exactly that.

I was still in that state of wishing that I'd never ventured away from Symi. I'd been cocooned on the island. In summer, I'd been lulled by daily swims in the blue sea, and eating fish caught moments before they were eaten, and, in winter, by taking long walks up into the hillsides that surrounded the port, just as I had done on Hydra. Drinking the local wine and cloudy ouzo that tasted like licorice added to the soothing effect of the island.

Often the purpose of those walks, especially in winter, was to visit the monasteries—churches, really—that were never used. They had been built by men who had made a pact with God when they were forced to leave the island to find work. They prayed that if they found wealth enough in the outside world, they would repay Him by building Him a home. There were many such churches on this nearly deserted island. They remained glistening white in the sun, empty of everything but the spirit of God and the spirit of hope. I'd wandered from one to another, fascinated by their beauty and their silence, all the while looking down upon the sea far beneath me.

There had been a young German man who had travelled to Symi. Jean Claude and I befriended him. He was in transit, moving aimlessly from one country to another. Travel was his only goal. He insisted on keeping to this purpose, and for that reason he forced himself to leave the island eventually. We went to the port to see him depart on the ferry to Rhodes, and as it pulled away we could hear him shout "J'aurais du rester"—"I should have stayed." We laughed. We'd spent so many wine-soaked nights telling him that he should remain. In the months and even years ahead, this phrase would resound in my head like a pounding Greek chorus.

But the woman in the deserted London airport was waiting for me. I responded to her politely officious greeting, and we set off together. I don't know where in London she lived, but I do know that I slept on her couch for the rest of that short night

The next morning after a fitful night's sleep, the lady made me a traditional English breakfast of eggs with yolks the color of bright orange, accompanied by tiny grilled tomatoes. My spirits lifted. She then drove me down to the village outside of London where Dorothy and Glenn had found work as house parents in a boys' boarding school. Dorothy had planned their future well. They were both content and happy. I was to stay with them until they were free to drive me to London, where I would be introduced to their Australian friends and handed over to their care. This was indeed adventure. But inwardly I felt the way a child in foster care must feel, moving from one home to another, hoping for a welcome.

Upon arrival at the boarding school, the woman dropped me at the back entrance and disappeared. I never saw her again. The newly formed family was waiting for me and quickly ushered me indoors and down a flight of stairs to what I later learned was the employees' living quarters. Dorothy and Glen had a small, underground warren of rooms that opened out onto a long corridor, which turned into my exercise run for the next week.

Because Dorothy and Glenn weren't allowed to have guests, they gave me strict orders to remain hidden. Secretly they brought me down meals from the dining room and left them before immediately returning to work "upstairs." I cowered in their flat like a cat who hides under a bed in a strange home and creeps out to eat the food left for her only after the coast is cleared of the very people who brought it.

I realized then that I hardly knew Dorothy and Glenn, not to mention England. They were taking a risk harboring me in their living quarters, bringing me food, and introducing me to their friends. They did not really know me either, but they were kind and caring, at least for that period of time. When their next day off occurred, which turned out to be one long week away, they dispatched me to London.

* * *

That day arrived, and we squeezed into their old Fiat "Deux Chevaux," with the newly born baby. I was taken to a large, rundown "row" house in Stockwell, a working class district in southwest London, where Dorothy presented me to her friends. They were a motley group mostly in their twenties and thirties and included not only Australians but also a young

Chinese man, an Englishwoman, a Scotsman and some Irish. There were also several cats.

No less motley were their accommodations. The house in which they lived had once been a grand dwelling but it had been divided into bedrooms known as bed-sits, the shorthand British term for a room that contained a bed. In that room one could sit, eat, or even cook meals if there was a single gas burner. Kitchen, toilet and bath were shared. The building had three floors and two large landings, one of which had been transformed into a galley kitchen for the upstairs rooms.

There was also a ground floor apartment cut in half to make two units. It consisted of its own shared kitchen and bath and one bedroom in each unit. One of the rooms even had a fireplace and certainly was the better half of what once had been the drawing room. This was indeed luxury. When I finally got my first paycheck six weeks after my arrival, a tenant was leaving the room with the fireplace. This was luck. I assumed that the room would be coveted by the others who lived in the building but I need not have worried. It gradually became clear to me that these people, who had travelled so far from their homes, hardly left their rooms except to go to the local Laundromat, grocery store, flea market or pub.

They huddled together like brave refugees and sometimes like timid hostages. It was enough for them to be a part of this small, loyal community of exiles squeezed under one roof. If they did leave the house during the day, they scurried back at night alone. Some of them went out to work; others seemed to have small independent incomes and didn't need to work. With few exceptions, they neither wanted nor felt they needed contact with the outside world.

In Stockwell, in 1973, that world consisted mostly of white, working-class British with a smattering of Irish, who had come to find work that was not available in Ireland because of the uprisings pitting Catholics against Protestants. There were a few upper-class professionals who had bought houses identical to ours and were setting out to gentrify the neighborhood.

The house I was to live in for the next two years sat on the corner of a small row of identical buildings. A short walkway that led to the front stairs had a bare patch of earth on either side. When the house had been inhabited by a single family this area would have been a garden, but now it smelled of cat urine mixed with leaking gas. Entering the front hallway, one got the impression that much was going on in a small amount of space. This was true.

On the first floor, the residents named Glendenning and Christopher shared one large bed-sit. Christopher was Chinese and had come to London from Singapore to study voice. He could be heard singing operatic scales at any time of the day. Though he and Glendenning were both gay, they were not lovers. Christopher was small, and his head was set way back on his neck. He walked erectly, his chest pushed out in front him, making him resemble a pigeon who had swallowed its own round cage. He was full of energy and purpose and decidedly out spoken with a cultivated and clipped British voice.

His roommate was very different. Glendenning was Australian and inclined to melancholy, but when he talked, it was with warmth and interest. He disappeared one day after telling us that he was thinking of taking a trip back to his native Australia. He returned two days later with a foolish grin and an April Fools' Day attitude explaining that he had purposefully scheduled his return to England the moment he touched ground in Australia. He wanted to know what forty-eight hours of flying felt like "just for the hell of it."

Maureen, who was also from Australia, shared the room opposite, with her cats and her many flea market finds. Although I never saw her leave her big rumpled bed, she was always dressed in shabby finery that seemed to blend in with her disheveled, mouse-colored hair. She and Christopher loved to chat conspiratorially, yet they always welcomed me whenever I dared venture into their rooms between job interviews or when suffering bouts of loneliness which I did when I had no interviews to attend or when I had to take my clothes to the neighborhood launderette.

There, once again alone, I could not help but listen to the lively chattering of others around me. They all seemed to belong to each other. They knew what laundry soap to use and how the machines worked. They had someone at home waiting for them, wondering why it had taken them so long or asking if they needed help folding the laundry.

I wore a long, muted, diagonally striped cotton Gypsy-like skirt in those days. I felt in need of a wash myself, and I often sat on the long bench between the two aisles of washing machines imagining myself immersed in suds spinning endlessly around and around and around in the contained space of an aluminum cylinder.

There was no container for me. I don't think I realized at that point that I was feeling depressed, nor did I connect my mood with the fact that it had taken me an hour to leave the house once I had packed up my laundry. I kept looking in the mirror to check my face before I went out in public. Although this sounds melodramatic, I think now it was to check to see if I was really there, that I existed.

I was aware of a constant sensation in my stomach, a feeling of its being hollow, along with a quiet dread of saying or doing something wrong. I resolved to return to my mother's teachings, to say nothing and to watch to see how others behave, then imitate it. I also found that, more and more, I wanted to stay indoors, but I had to get out for job interviews. It was fortunate that I had to. Otherwise, I would have made myself even more invisible.

My room—or rather my shared bed—was located under the eaves in the attic. It was all the space I had for those many long weeks before I was able to find work. Velda, whose bed it was, offered to share her bed with me, not only because she was generous, but also because she was sometimes out of it, sleeping elsewhere. She was six feet tall, dark-haired, gregarious, full-breasted and generous to everyone. She was the lone English person living in the house and spoke with a sharply clipped British accent.

Out of necessity and somewhat shamefully, I had accepted her kind offer of the bed, but I would not let myself even mildly invade her space. I felt like an intruder, like someone in a charity ward. It was a unique situation for me, the first time I recognized how humiliating it felt to need something I couldn't supply for myself. It made me want to hide in corners, ghost-like, unseen. I did not want to impose on anyone.

Velda was employed as a secretary in some sort of political office. At night, she worked overtime by acting as an escort for these same politicians with whom she worked during the day, accompanying them to dinner, night spots, and often to their hotel rooms afterwards. There were also occasions, however, when Velda needed her own bed at night to bring these gentlemen to it. I had to be out of there; three would obviously have been a crowd. I would then become a guest of Margaret, whose twin-bedded room was just across the hall.

Margaret didn't mind my presence as long as the visits were just occasional. Although she kept mostly to herself, she loved to tell me about her work as the switchboard operator at the Royal Opera House in Convent Garden and to talk about the village in Scotland that she came from. At that time, Covent Garden was a quietly bustling part of London where people came to attend the opera and to eat in the restaurants or to have a drink in the many pubs. There was a very beautiful and lush flower market there, but not much else in the way of commerce, as it is today with its shops and malls and cafes. It felt to me like a space apart from the rest of London, where I could look at the pretty people and the flowers and listen to the glorious music at the opera and forget, for that time, the pressure I felt at having to get work.

For me to be with Margaret was to be at peace for a little while. She looked at, and listened deeply to her world, small as it was. She wanted no other. She walked with a pronounced limp that did not diminish the twinkle in her beautiful lavender eyes framed by soft tendrils of curly reddish hair falling from a spinsterish topknot. Margaret extended invitations to me to attend dress rehearsals at the Royal Opera House, where I remember seeing a stunning rendition of Madame Butterfly on a day when I had no job interviews to go to.

These people kept me pasted together while I tried to navigate my way through the fogs of London. This was sharing. This was being there for one another without asking any questions, without making any judgments, without letting curiosity infringe on good manners. Even though we were strangers to one another, this was my family. They were enabling me to survive. They were people who at one time or another had themselves been humbled by life. They watched me from the sidelines with vigilance and a readiness to protect. They knew that it was my moment to be humbled by all that I needed and might not be able to provide for myself.

As much as I may have gotten in their way, they never wavered in their acceptance of me. In retrospect, I have wondered if it was not boredom, due to a lack of activity in their own lives, that made them so giving to me. But I cannot ever know the truth of that, and it seems mean-spirited of me to take such benign generosity and twist it into something negative.

I was barely able to reflect on this state of affairs at the time because I was so immersed in trying to stay afloat myself. My stash of sterling was dwindling, and I had many interviews that led me nowhere. I had to learn that just because these people were speaking English, I would not necessarily understand what they were saying. I had a new climate to adjust to. My clothes were flimsy and clung to me through one bout of flu after another. It was a long time before I realized that, just because the temperature read mild, there was a wet, rawness to the air that undermined my immune system.

As with the food. It was mostly wet and soggy, or so it seemed to me. I learned to eat only what I liked, which brought me back to having the bad nutritional judgment of a child. In fact, I felt like a child more and more. One who had been allowed to be outdoors playing for far too long. Darkness was coming, and no one was there to claim me. I was learning to panic.

But I did finally get work, thanks to my master of social work degree. I was to be a social service social worker employed by the Royal Borough of Kensington and Chelsea. The district is home to the Queen's palace, known as Kensington Palace, along with many other smaller residences belonging to various members of the royal family. There were also large majestic houses set back from the road that were now divided up into bed-sits. These I visited daily.

In retrospect I can see that it was my job to be kind, humane, non-judgmental, and helpful to those who needed assistance. All the psychology that I had learned in graduate school and for the reason I was hired, was not required. The elderly Lady P., for example, needed to have her hangover cured. She would make a phone call to the social service office and I was dispatched. It was my job to take her in a taxi, paid for by the department, in order to find her fresh raw meat to eat. She insisted that this was the only way she could get herself back together again. She was crotchety and treated me like the servant I was, making no distinction between me, the civil servant, and those house servants she had employed in her better days.

She and her conspicuously gay husband lived across the hall from one another on the top floor of a large white pillared house that had been converted into bed-sits and was far less shabby than the one I lived in. Their separate rooms were paid for by the Royal Borough because although the couple were legally married, they refused to share a room. They continued to drink together—and to fight together. I became their de facto referee rather than their couples' therapist as they were always wearing nightclothes and were either on their way to getting drunk or recovering from a bout of heavy drinking.

Then there was Mrs. S. She was wheelchair-bound and corpulent. She, too, lived in a bed-sit under the eaves paid for by the department. I was there to listen to her life story, again and again. She had been married to one of the biggest manufacturers of salt in Great Britain. They had met in a hospital when he was near death and she had been the beautiful young nurse who had brought him back to life. The story goes that they married and continued to be very much in love until he died. He had children from a previous marriage, however, who balked at this union. Mrs. S. got cut out of his will, yet somehow seemed to harbor no grudge.

I had been trained to look for signs of underlying rage in people who had problems with obesity. But Mrs. S. defied all the literature on the subject. I couldn't find even a trace of anger so perpetually jolly was she. Because she was down on her luck and penniless, the Royal Borough took care of her, and she in turn took care of me. After I made the long steep climb up the stairs to her single room at the top, she always had the makings of tea ready for me, water boiling on the single gas burner she was allowed in her room. At her side was a small table containing biscuits that she offered along with an insistence that I stay well past the time allotted for the visit. It was hard to deny such caring when I felt a stranger in my newly adopted country. I have often wondered who, out of each of us, received the most benefit.

At that time the British placed foster children in boarding schools rather than in private homes with foster parents, as we do in the United States. In that way, the children are at least given an excellent education that well equips them for life after leaving care at age nineteen. It was part of my job to visit one such school in order to offer individual sessions for any boy who was having emotional problems.

I had a rickety old Morris Minor, a tiny four-door sedan with a floor so rusted out that I could see the roadway beneath my feet. The boys, however, loved it. They would watch for my arrival and run out of the building when they saw me drive through the heavy iron gates. They swarmed into the car and climbed up on the hood, the running boards, the roof. "Please, Miss, may I see you?" they pleaded. "Please, Miss?"

They lined up at the door of the office I was given for the day's visit. Their problems ranged from being too quiet to bullying to being bullied to being a jokester. Except for the boy being bullied, they showed no overt signs of distress. And they seemed to delight in being in the company of someone who would listen to them. We sat and chatted and joked together. It was easy to give, and what I could give was happily received.

Was it enough? Of course not. But for those moments, there was an acknowledgment of how special they were, and of how special they made me feel clamoring—half in jest and half in need—to see me. I was touched by their obvious adoration of me and by their delight at my visit. They lifted my spirits and took the fright out of the long drive back to London on the M4 where cars were whizzing past me at seventy miles an hour.

The system was rarely abused, but I do remember one occasion in which I spent an entire day on the phone pleading with a father in Zambia to take back his fourteen-year-old daughter. The child of a top official in the Zambian government had been put on a plane by her father and told to declare herself abandoned when she arrived in England. By doing this, the father thought, she would become a ward of the British and be placed by them in boarding school, something he couldn't afford. But the Royal Borough would not have it.

I told the father that we could not place the girl as he was her rightful guardian and the family did not live in England. I pleaded with him to come to collect her or to send her money for a plane ticket so she could return to him. He staunchly refused. This attitude stretched the limits of British generosity, although in the end, the government relented slightly and paid for the girl's plane ticket back to her father. He had had the best of intentions in temporarily abandoning his daughter to the care of the Queen Mother, who would have educated her royally.

It soon became my turn to be educated, at least emotionally. Having some income freed me to reflect on what I had done as I no longer had to worry about merely surviving. I was earning very little, about two thousand pounds sterling a year, amounting to about $4000 at that time, but it didn't matter to me or to anyone else. We all had about the same amount of money, it seemed. We could go to the theater from time to time as it was not expensive, or clubbing every once in a while, and certainly to the pub for a drink whenever we liked.

I was beginning to feel less of an outsider. In fact, I was feeling more comfortable than I had ever felt in America. I had no answers for why that was so. I was appreciative of the British for their politeness, their regard for others, their understatement. Effortlessly, I understood their humor. I admired the sharp, precise way they spoke. I had not realized that I was imitating them until on one brief visit home, my sister said in shock, "You have an English accent!" Quietly but surely, I was melding with the British.

I felt closer to them than I did to my own family since the time of my mother's remarriage twenty years earlier. I realized later that part of the familiarity I felt living abroad had to do with my mother's parents, who had fled Russia before World War I. My mother frequently left me in their care while she was shopping or cleaning or when she had simply had enough of me. In those days after my father's death and before her remarriage seven years later, her patience was slight. She was depressed—burdened by fears of not having enough money, of being preyed upon by peeping Toms, of being left alone to raise two young children. My grandmother welcomed me with games and hair brushing and nail-polishing fun.

The home of my grandparents, located on a busy road in the town of Morristown, N.J. was an old fake yellow brick, three-story structure with a wrap-around porch dressed up with my grandmother's rocking chair, a bench for visitors, and a large lavender-colored wisteria shrub twisting around the porch pillars. It felt distinctly European. From the faded red flowered oil cloth cover on the antique kitchen table to the bare, highly polished wood floors covered by scatter rugs, their home was filled with antiques of every kind.

In the backyard were stables where my grandfather kept curly maple chests of drawers, end tables and chairs. He often picked out the best of them to keep in his house and grumbled when my grandmother urged him to show those pieces to the antique dealers who came from New York City to buy from him. Antiques were their business, but my grandfather hated to sell things, so attached to their beauty he had become.

Bric-a-brac was my grandmother's domain, and fragile porcelain figurines were placed in an antique corner cupboard in the small living room overly filled with a Victorian sofa and chairs. An ever-changing display, my grandmother sold whatever she could and the rest became a staple of my childhood, for example, the iron terrier dog that now sits on my floor to stop the wind from slamming the door shut.

It was said that my grandfather, a quiet gentleman, spoke seven languages when he was forced to speak, but that was mostly for business purposes. To supplement his modest income, he bought muskrat and beaver and other animals from the local trappers and sold their pelts to furriers in the city. No matter that he was skinning their fur from their bodies which were suspended from a rope tacked to the low-ceilinged basement, or going to auction sales at estates in the surrounding countryside, he always wore a tie and three piece suit covering many other layers of clothing as if to keep the cold of Russia at bay.

I listened in awe when he spoke Italian with his next-door neighbors, my grandparents' friends who taught him their language soon after his arrival in America in 1907, where he came to escape being conscripted into the Russian Army. I watched fascinated as he cut crusty Italian bread with a knife in one hand while he held the bread against his chest with the other.

But I did not make this connection between my past life and what was attracting me in the present one until well into my own analysis, which I began in England sometime in 1977. I had already been living there for four years. I was beginning to feel that I needed answers to questions like, "Why did I feel so at home in Europe? Why didn't I want to return to my family in America?" I did not want to change. I simply wanted to understand.

And this is exactly what I said to my analyst in that first session. I said it as though I knew exactly what I was doing. I did not know then that one cannot have understanding of something that has eluded them without that understanding, when it arrives, changing them. There is an infinitesimal shift when the old way of thinking is no longer imbedded within us, but instead lifts up its head as if to sniff the air for the first time. My analyst responded kindly by remaining silent. And thus began our relationship together.

Having become a psychoanalyst myself, I know how heart-rending it can be when a patient needs to repeat their destructive behavior. Freud called this behavior repetition compulsion. The positive side of such action is that through this repetition, we may be trying to gain mastery over destructive actions. It is often said that we must learn from our mistakes, and with guidance we often do. Or, if we feel the pain for long enough, we will correct our behavior.

The problem is that we have so many different ways of defending ourselves against emotional pain that we become immune to it. Psychoanalysts guide but should not instruct. There is a great, but subtle difference between the two. Patients must live out their own behavior until they understand viscerally, emotionally, and intellectually exactly what they are doing and why they are doing it.

In my relationships, I was making the same mistakes over and over again. As soon as one inappropriate relationship ended, I would begin another. This was my way of distracting myself from feeling the hurt and pain and loneliness. Bloodied and exhausted though I was, I could not see my way out of this pattern. In fact, there was something so engaging about being miserable that I must not have wanted to leave that state, much as I knew consciously that I had to. "Misery loves company" often means the need for more misery to keep the rest of the misery company until an entire brigade of miseries is assembled and we become so depressed that the only place to take that brigade, short of suicide, is to the psychiatric ward of a hospital, where one need do nothing anymore. Everything is taken care of. No worries.

Luckily, understanding dawned on me before that had to happen. Maybe part of it was because I did register my analyst's behavior through the throes of my own. Sometimes I could feel her flinch at my distress. She hurt for me; she felt for me. I could feel that. And I began to hurt for myself. Even though I could not see her unless I turned my head to the right side of the moss green velvet couch where I lay and gazed slightly back at her, I could sense her discomfort. I did not turn around frequently because it required too much physical effort to move. I did not want to move.

Whether it was anger or despair or the shock of discovery or simply ranting because at last I had someone to listen to me, I wanted to go on feeling my emotions into infinity. When I cried, I never thought that I'd stop even though I knew that by the end of the fifty minutes I'd have to wipe mascara off my face and drive back through the London roads. Life goes on at varying levels when one undergoes an analysis. Past, present and future all come together during the analytical hour. The child is there alongside the adult. Sometimes an infant peers over the top of her crib, and sometimes it is the frightened six-year-old with the painful earache back again. My analyst held all of these incarnations together for me while I was falling apart.

Well into my second year of analysis, I continued to make all the wrong decisions for myself. My analyst suffered them in empathic silence. Only occasionally did her pain become so great that she needed to protest and would tell me what I should or should not do. But I hardly heard her response as anything more than a distant rumble. I paid it no mind. How I flinched when my own patients—years later—would show me their mutilated skin after a cutting spree. How I could feel my anger at them rise and then have to control it because this was about them and not about my feelings, however instinctive and understandable they were.

My analyst metaphorically held my hand through all of my pain, much the way my own mother did when I was a child sitting in the dentist's chair. She neither looked away nor went away. We were both in it together. I knew that she cared. I knew that she trusted me to emerge from the experience intact. Her knowing silence, combined with her unwavering presence, was kindness at its most profound.

By remaining in England, I grew out of needing to return to Greece. This was not a decision I made consciously. But at a certain point it became too difficult to live both lives. I could not take time off work to visit Greece. I did not have money enough for travel. I was beginning to get some perspective on the life I had lived with Jean Claude and I wanted this new one to take me further away from that. I remained in England for fifteen years.

The gifts of kindness that I was given by the British, and especially the kindness given to me from my analyst, changed me forever. I'd like to think that I've brought them back to America with me. I'd like to think that I have passed them on to my patients and to those around me. I'd like to think that they are that cat in the room that graces it with her beauty. But the truth is that I do not think about them any more than I think about breathing. Anyway, it feels like that.

CHAPTER SIX:

THE FRENCH COUNT

As a social worker and as a psychotherapist, one is frequently confronted with moral dilemmas. Almost always, it seems, ethical decisions have to be made in the time that it takes to write one's signature on a legal document affecting the life of someone you have only just met. Reason can conflict with feeling and with intuition, but danger often abounds. And sometimes, something has to be done quickly. This is especially so when the client or patient is behaving as if he might harm himself or someone else. There is a technical phrase for these situations used by those in the helping professions which is, "Is the patient or client a danger to himself or to others?" And if so, immediate measures must be taken to put that person out of harm's way.

My first encounter of this kind was when I was working as a social worker for the Royal Borough of Kensington and Chelsea and before I ever thought of training as a psychoanalyst. In this neighborhood, the Borough footed the bill for a great many fallen gentry. It was there that I began my career in earnest as I encountered the first moral dilemma of my budding career. It involves a tragic story about a French count in his early seventies who was living in London in a spacious and elegant flat in one of those grand old townhouses in busy Kensington. But this time there was not a bed-sit in sight, as the neighborhood was posh and his address a good one. There were simply two or three other apartments clustered around the count's.

One day during the summer of my first year working for the agency, a staff member of the Royal Borough of Kensington and Chelsea received a phone call from one of the count's neighbors saying that they feared for his safety because he seemed to be growing senile and had once or twice left on the gas of his cook stove. Gas had permeated the building's stairwell and corridors, the neighbor had added, and could someone please come around to check things out before they were all killed by the count and his live-in mistress, who was also aged and certainly demented.

I was asked to go round to make a preliminary assessment. I spoke some French, having been taught it in high school and college, and then encouraged to speak it while living with the French painter and entertaining his friends. Although I spoke it poorly, I understood the culture behind the words very well, making up for what I missed in speech. I was also that American who had been graduate schooled in such things as mental health diagnosis. I was the obvious "learned" choice. After all, my American education in social work was the reason that the Royal Borough had hired me.

The Count, I was told, was about seventy years old and clearly down on his luck. He had no relatives living in England. He had been divorced from his French wife, who was living in France and had been rebuffed by his children many years earlier because of his liaison with his mistress.

I had known French counts before. The French painter and I had lived for a time in Paris, where his patrons included a count and a countess. Although France no longer has royalty, they could boast of royal lineage and so continued to use their royal titles, along with their inherited properties.

It turned out, incidentally, that they too had an aristocratic marriage riddled with problems. Their solution was to keep the marriage intact because divorce would have created bigger problems concerning the distribution of a great deal of inherited wealth. They opted for the typical French solution turned to in such a situation. The count took a mistress. The countess ignored the other woman's existence and went off to church praying ever harder for the salvation of their souls—and the strength to bear her husband until death should part them.

As a result, I was familiar with this kind of accommodation. Now in my early thirties and having lived in Europe for six years mainly because of my love for Jean Claude, I accepted this code of ethics as being part of the norm. When I was told about the Count, I did not judge him, nor his decision to have an English mistress, and not even a young and pretty vacant one but a woman his own age who was, according to his neighbors, slipping into dementia even more quickly than her lover.

My office, on the other hand, was spartan—one big room with about twelve social workers' desks crowded together on the first floor of what was once was a large home at the bottom of Notting Hill Gate. I walked to the Count's home, which was a few blocks away. The outer door of the building resembled 10 Downing Street. The door was unlocked, and I was able to let myself in and walk up a short flight of carpeted stairs to arrive at their flat without having to announce myself beforehand. When I rang the bell to their apartment, it was answered by the so called "madame de la maison" or "mademoiselle", I shall never know which.

She was tall and elegant in the way that the flat was, and clearly out of her mind. She mistook me for somebody's daughter, some long-lost relative returned at last from her stay in Belize. Even the Count, whom she led him by the hand into the entrance hall to meet me, was obviously exasperated by her mistaken perception.

He in turn led me into the drawing-room, which was furnished sparsely but impeccably with solid looking furniture upholstered in heavy dark green velvet. Also velvet were the draperies, partially drawn over the tall half-open windows that looked out onto the busy street below. Sound was extinguished by them in the mid-morning sunshine. A stream of dust particles filtered through the light coming in from the window and caught my attention, taking it away for an instant, from the handsome white-haired, elegant, gallant Count standing before me.

He was compact and well-proportioned in the muscular way of the French who have never set foot in a gym, and was neatly dressed in a Noel-Coward-like smoking jacket. He was exceedingly welcoming and seemed relieved that I was there, as if I could protect him from this woman, his mistress, who had clearly lost her mind. The Count had had enough. He told me how he had sacrificed his ancestral home, his former wife and his children for love of her. He did not fill me in on the details of this romance, and I regret that I shall never know them; but he did express, albeit very subtly, sadness.

It was now apparent that he felt he had made the wrong choice. His four children would not speak to him. His wife would have nothing to do with him, and in fact had robbed him of a great chunk of his inheritance. And this woman, with whom he was living, was a constant source of worry and irritation.

"Yes, she needs to be put somewhere else," were his words. "Yes, she needs to be taken care of. I can no longer do it."

When I finally broached the reason for my visit, the Count replied, "Gas? What escaping gas? Never!" Then he added even more emphatically, "They are liars, those neighbors. They have never liked us. No. There is no gas. No. None at all."

"Pas du tout," he said with finality.

In fact, I could smell something, but I could not be sure what it was. We were in the kitchen, where he had escorted me after I told him of the neighbor's complaint. I could see that the kitchen looked neat if not clean. Obviously, there was not a lot of cooking going on. Was there a slight smell of gas? Possibly.

With that, we returned to the foyer where we said good-bye, but not before I received an invitation from him to return promptly. We had been speaking in French, something that seemed to endear me to him. It was obvious that my presence inspired in him a spark that lit into a flirtation, even admiration. I could speak French, and I could save him. Or so he thought.

I returned to the office to report my findings. My supervisor told me that I had to return the next day to continue my assessment, to keep an eye on the gas—and let the neighbors know that we were investigating the situation.

A few days later, I again let myself in through the main door, walked up the flight of heavily carpeted stairs and turned the handle of the bell beside the great wooden door. It opened instantly as though the Count had planted himself there to wait for my return. There he stood, this time wearing tweeds and tie and looking more like a British count than a French one, but a Count indeed. He was smiling broadly and bent to take and kiss my hand.

"Enter," he said. "You will see that I am alone. She is gone. She was taken away by her niece and nephew. They came for her, I know not how, and they said that they would look after her. Mademoiselle, I am so relieved. She is gone. She will be well taken care of."

This time I did smell gas in the foyer, and after speaking a few words in French in response to his feelings of relief, I asked to be taken to the kitchen. He escorted me there happily. I could feel my heart sink as I sniffed the air, thicker now with the unmistakable foul scent of escaping gas. I begged his pardon but nonetheless blithely asked, "Could I please have a match to light the pilot?" I hoped that my casual tone would camouflage my fear.

"Certainly, Mademoiselle," he replied in French, "You are so kind to do this for me."

With trepidation and with matchbox in hand, I moved towards the stove, found the pilot light, reached as far back from the stove as I could, struck a match, and with the longest reach I could muster, touched the lit match to the stove. Oomph! The gas lit. I quickly reduced the flame. We were good.

For now. For today, we were O.K. Because of my visit that day, his life had probably been saved. But I would not be able to visit his flat daily. I could not go there on weekends to check on him. I could do nothing but return to the office and report what had happened.

My orders were to return to the Count. I was instructed to tell him that we could provide care for him in a home for the elderly so that he need not worry about forgetting to turn off the gas on the stove. In fact, he need not worry about anything now that he would be taken care of by his adopted country. If he refused this offer, I was to telephone our psychiatrist to give him a head's up. He would then arrive to make an assessment, and if it matched my observations, we were legally bound to take the Count into our care. We would do this by calling for an ambulance to take the Count to a facility like a psychiatric hospital or perhaps an old-age home, whichever the Royal Borough of Kensington and Chelsea had in mind for him.

The next day, I reluctantly returned to his flat. He was delighted to see me so soon again, bent to kiss my hand and invited me once again to move into the drawing-room where the dust motes flew around the heavy furniture like butterflies around a flower bed.

I braced myself. As quickly as I could, I delivered the speech that I had been instructed to give. I said that we were concerned about him and that he was in danger of harming himself or others because he kept forgetting to turn off the gas. By law, I continued, he needed to be protected from killing himself (or others, I repeated for emphasis) and we were offering to move him to a place of safety under our care.

"This cannot be," he replied heatedly, "This will not be. There is nothing wrong. I harm no one. Those neighbors who speak to you are idiots." His voice escalated. "I will not go. You cannot make me go. I refuse to go."

It was early morning. He was still wearing his neatly pressed striped silk pajamas. I could feel myself break into small fragments that I knew I must piece together if I was to do my job. I remembered the orders that I had received the day before and made an enormous effort to push my shattered feelings aside in order to employ all the reason that I could muster for this situation.

I repeated all the good intentions the British were putting on offer to the Count, but as he was having none of it, I went on to say that unfortunately this decision was neither mine nor his to make. He became unintelligible, or maybe it was my own inability to make sense of his words, as I was using all of my concentration to try to hold myself together so that I could perform well for the Royal Borough. I felt badly for him as I did not think that he was senile at all. I felt badly for me because his rage frightened me. I felt badly for his neighbors who were being put at risk because of his carelessness or was his forgetfulness a forerunner of dementia? And I liked the man. I didn't want to cause him distress.

He must have said something about going to his room to dress, or maybe he just stomped off in a rage, but in any case, I found myself alone in the drawing room. There was a telephone, and I reached for it so I could call my office and tell them to move ahead with the proceedings.

Within minutes, it seemed, the psychiatrist appeared, having been driven to the count's home by the ambulance men. From the window, I could see the vehicle parked in the street below. I watched as the psychiatrist approached the outer door and entered the building soundlessly. Seconds later he arrived at our doorstep, which was now the Count's and mine, or so it now seemed to me.

At the sound of our voices discussing his "case," the Count emerged from his bedroom and before I could make the appropriate introductions, demanded to know who was this man talking to me. The psychiatrist asked him if they could speak privately in the next room. The Count, whose dignity and good nature apparently had been restored by his renewed resolve and some fresh clothing, agreed. The two men moved into the drawing room with the dust butterflies while I moved into the kitchen to find an untended flame flickering on the gas stove.

After half an hour, I heard the Count screaming. The assessment was completed. His refusal of our offerings was apparent. I forced myself to enter the scene of battle, as if my presence would make a difference. Unsurprisingly, it did not. Before we knew it, the Count was apoplectic and in danger of having a stroke.

It was as if the idea of banishment from his present home had made him recall the banishment from his home in France, something his former wife had insisted upon many years before. His own guilt and generous nature had made him agreeable to such an anathema. Now he was facing the very real trauma of being forced out of his home and carted off to somewhere unknown. No wonder he was screaming.

The men in white coats appeared from the ambulance on the street having heard the commotion from the partially open window in the drawing room. Syringes also appeared. The men approached the Count and he, in turn, fought back by striking them with his fists. They tried to fend him off, but he began kicking their legs and biting their outstretched arms. From somewhere there appeared a strait jacket. Two men held it and descended on him, while a third wielding a syringe moved in closer. I found myself rooting for the ambulance men because I did not want the Count to have a stroke.

This ghastly scene needed an ending, and hard as the count fought, he was no match for three sturdy and practiced men. At last they enclosed him in the stiff white jacket as gently as they could. The Count's head flailed back and forth atop the vest until it did no longer. The syringe had found its mark.

I walked behind the medics as they headed out the door and down the stairs to put him carefully into the ambulance. They did not need me. I needed them. I needed something to do. A sensation of emptiness was overwhelming me. I dreaded going back up to that flat to close the door. And besides, I felt that I needed to remain at his side until he arrived at the hospital to which they were now taking him. He had proven by his uncontrollable behavior that he was a danger to himself. The psychiatrist had given the order. He would remain in the hospital while further assessments were made.

Two days later, I went to the hospital to visit him. My heart still ached and my mind was still conflicted. "Was he a danger to himself, or were we a danger to him?" I kept asking myself.

The nurse brought him over to me in the waiting room where I had been sitting. He was wearing hospital pajamas and a stiff institutional white robe. This time there was no hand kiss, no welcoming smile. He looked as though the light had gone out of him. The charm and the sweet and gentle nature had evaporated, to be replaced by an old man, walking limply towards me like one of the living dead. He had not forgotten his manners, however, and he greeted me with a slight bow of his head. He then looked up and fixed his eyes on mine. I was unable to look away. With their clarity and strength, his eyes alone presented a startling contrast to the rest of him. All that I had left to give him was the courtesy of a similar response; and I remember thinking, if he can weather this, so can I.

He then spoke to me, words I shall never forget. Slowly, and deliberately spacing out each word he said, "I never should have let you into my home."

The words struck me like the sound of a death knell. I knew he was right. It was my turn to bow my head. Tears dripped down my face and splashed onto the highly polished floor beneath our feet. This time I could invoke no reason. I sensed that he wanted me to leave. I did so, walking as he had, with a lifeless limp.

One week later, I got word from my superiors that he was dead. He was seventy-one years old. I was to go the funeral as the Borough's representative under whose auspices he was being cremated. That is how I came to be with him again, but this time in a nondescript funeral home in a nearby suburb of London. I was the only person there.

I watched as the urn moved down the conveyor belt after the burning of his body had been completed. I watched and wondered where those ashes would go. They were not mine to take. I did not know what representatives of social service agencies did in such cases. This time I had been given no instructions. I waited a long time alongside the elegant urn once it reached the bottom of the sturdy aluminum belt. The day was clear and bright. There was utter silence as the Count and I came to another standstill.

CHAPTER SEVEN:

AN APOLOGY TO LEONARD

I met the singer Leonard Cohen on the Greek island of Hydra in the winter of 1968 when I was twenty-six years old and still married to my first husband. He was twenty-seven years old and had read Leonard's recent novel, "Beautiful Losers," an erotic tragedy mixing the sacred and the profane, and was so impressed by it that he insisted that we travel to that island, where Cohen, a Canadian, was then living, to find him. I didn't know anything about Leonard, his songs or his poetry at that time. I was not told more, and I did not think to ask.

We were young and solvent. We set sail for England on October 1, 1967. The members of the Mamas and the Papas, a famous folk-rock group, were also on board the ocean liner, and we felt, rightly, that our lives were just beginning. My husband, a successful short story writer turned successful comedy writer, had his agent at the William Morris Agency who forwarded money as needed. And since I had completed my graduate work at New York University a few months before we left, and could easily delay finding employment until our unscheduled return; we were free to travel wherever we wanted.

Our first stop was London, where we were going to study Transcendental Meditation as the Beatles practiced it. England, being the birthplace of the Beatles, had become a mecca for prospective meditators. I hadn't given meditation much thought, but I was a Beatles fan, and my husband was eager to learn meditation, and so was I.

In November when we arrived, the deep yellow fog so characteristic of the city had begun to be less of a presence, but not yet the reminders of war. Even in 1968, people still spoke of the systematic and relentless bombing of Britain, and especially London, as though it had happened yesterday. For us, in the United States, who had been born at the war's beginning, the event hardly existed except as a fact of history. I had uncles who had returned from the war, but they never spoke about it. My mother frequently told me that my father had been terribly disappointed when he was rejected by the draft because of his rheumatic heart, but her emphasis was not on the war but on his ill health and his feelings of being emasculated by the draft board's decision.

In England I was jolted into remembrance. There was a feeling in the air that the British had come through something terrible, and had not only survived it, but had been extraordinarily brave and resourceful to have done so. Even though the war had been over for more than two decades, they had not put behind them their bravest moments and wanted to tell young Americans like us all about them.

Proudly and sometimes even humorously, we were regaled with stories told by people who were the ages of our parents. One woman who owned a bed and breakfast where we stayed on our arrival in Southampton, showed us her bomb shelter. It was a small space under the eaves of the stairwell that we ascended each night to go to our room. Open on one side, it was not the safest of places, but the woman had made it safe during the war by grabbing the biggest pot lid that she had and covering her backside with it while staring bent over facing the opposite wall. The story was told to us in good fun, the woman herself bending over to demonstrate how her do-it-herself bomb shelter had worked, but this time she was laughing and unafraid. The expression "cover your ass" had never seemed so accurate.

Despite the city's efforts to clean the air, London looked grim and gray to me. Londoners, however, were jolly, particularly those whom we met as fellow meditators. Some of them had been trained to teach meditation by their Indian counterparts. Great respect was given to the mantra, a set of syllables individualized for each student and repeated until the meditator's thoughts were gently and naturally obliterated and the desired meditating state was reached. I recall sitting on the floor in one of the rooms of a large house located in Central London used as headquarters for Transcendental Meditation and trying to work with my mantra. We were told never to tell anyone else what it was. It felt like keeping the secret of Santa Claus from a child, but awestruck as we were, we obeyed.

My husband asked one of the meditators if he thought that meditation had made a difference in his life. The meditator's quick reply was, "Well if you like feeling the breeze on your face, you will like it." I don't know if meditation had that effect on me, but I do know that I started listening — really listening—to what my husband was saying, and surprisingly I did not like much of it.

Suddenly it seemed to me that his characteristic child-like excitement, which had always been so charming, was really phony, and that it was used as a way of distancing himself from people. He could dazzle them with his cleverness, his sense of humor, his ability to be articulate, but I was beginning to sense that there was no weight behind his words. Previously I had been in awe of his monologues, his dialogues, his sheer talent, but I began to wonder if this man that I had wed, wasn't all form and no content. Or was it feeling and emotion that was lacking? I didn't know. I still don't know, but I found myself shifting into a new awareness of him.

I was disappointed, and, I admit, silently judgmental. I had married a short story writer who had published his first story at age twenty-one in a highly reputable magazine and he was now a comedy writer for TV game shows and night club comedians. He himself seemed to ridicule his change of profession, but he never spoke openly about it, nor did I. The money he earned from writing for comedy was fun, but neither of us placed a value on having money.

Another change since having learned meditation was that the cityscape seemed brighter, more detailed, more connected to me rather than existing simply as a dreary backdrop. I liked meditation very much for many years and I took it very seriously, until I didn't. I was expecting to feel enlightened by the process, but no such feeling was obvious to me. As my personal life was unraveling, the reverse was true. Disenchantment with my husband was causing me to emotionally withdraw from him. Nevertheless I persevered. At best, transcendental meditation calmed me and made me feel less in a fog.

I did like meeting other meditators. They were mostly Greeks who had travelled to London as we had, to learn to meditate and to stay in that city until they did. One of them, a very serious young woman named Christina, became my friend. There was also a rich and handsome Greek about our age, who flitted in and out of our lives for a time. Like Christina, he spoke many languages perfectly, including English. He also dressed well, as did she, neatly, appropriately, elegantly. I never saw Christina in trousers or him in a T-shirt. They were both well-mannered with a touch of arrogance. They were sophisticated. They were "Continentals," the first I had known. My world was opening up.

Among our visitors was Ruth, the seventeen-year-old daughter of friends of ours in Woodstock, who arrived almost as soon as we had disembarked. With her parents' permission, she had decided to skip college in order to travel, and on her first day in London she arrived breathless at our bed and breakfast.

With cheeks glowing and eyes sparkling she tripped over her words as she told us that she had just met a great man that day and that she was in love. She had seen a demonstration going on in the street, and on an impulse, joined it. There she met him, the man she was so excited about. His name was Richard Rogers, and he was a British-Italian architect who with his partner, Renzo Piano, would go on to win a contest in 1971 to design the celebrated Pompidou Centre in Paris.

In time, Ruth and Richard married and, as far as I know, have stayed married all of these years. Back then, it seemed to me that hers was an instantaneous and explosive connection to Richard. It made me giddy with the thought that love could be so clear, simple, and filled with joy. Shortly after this encounter with Ruth, and when we felt that we had mastered meditation, we left London and headed for Greece aboard the fabled Orient Express.

* * *

When I look back on that period, the years 1967 and 1968 when my ex-husband and I were travelling together and before our break-up on Hydra in the late spring of 1968, I remember meeting many different people, strangers to us, but all of whom were searching for something. We would enter their lives in places where they allowed us to enter and then move onto the next encounter, the next train, the next hotel, the next country. We exchanged intimacies with these people whom we met along the way, like children playing musical chairs at a birthday party. Sometimes the experience was heady, like being on board the SS France with the Mamas and the Papas, whom we observed only from our deck chairs, but still, we felt close to the energy of Mama Cass which, in turn, seemed to move us nearer to the "real" person.

It wasn't that I was a celebrity chaser. That I have never been. I frequently confuse Robert de Niro with Al Pacino, both great actors but whose names I have been known to mix up. What I cherished most about these encounters, usually just a brief hour or two, or the length of a train journey, was the sense of seeing and being seen by another person, of connecting with these people. Of knowing that for the duration of that encounter I genuinely felt for them and with them and spoke the same language.

There was one train journey that I took alone, where the sensation of unity was an experience I shall never forget. It was after meeting Leonard, and after the break-up of my marriage on Hydra in the spring of 1968, and at the beginning of my relationship with the French painter.

I had been on a weeklong meditation retreat in a quaint hotel situated on beautiful Lago de Briase in the Dolomites of northern Italy and was heading to Munich to meet Jean Claude who was having an exhibition of his paintings there. I'd just had a hurried audience with the Maharishi himself, who met with each of the attendees before they left, as an added bonus to being on the retreat.

To reach the Maharishi, who was seated cross-legged on a dais, I had to walk down what seemed like a very long aisle separating rows of folding chairs in the hotel's conference room. When I was face to face with him, he looked at me for a long minute and then said only these words, "No more marijuana for you." Open-mouthed, I stared back at him. How did he know that I had ever smoked marijuana? It had been nearly two years since that summer between graduate school and sailing off for Europe when I treated myself to daily visits to the garden at the Cloisters in Washington Heights in a celebratory state of intoxication. I simply nodded and thanked him. I have not touched cannabis since.

Just after that meeting, on the train ride to Munich, I was placed in a compartment with five other people who mostly spoke German, a language whose sounds I only knew through my grandparents' having sometimes spoken in Yiddish. Suddenly I was understanding them and speaking to them in their language. I shall never forget the sense of elation I felt on that journey. Although I have tried to teach myself German since, that experience did not extend itself beyond the train's compartment. But the elation I felt, I feel again each time that I have connected to another human being and we sense that we have "seen" each other and "know" each other, if only briefly.

* * *

I remember meeting Leonard in a taverna that first winter on Hydra in 1968. He sat alone, a dark brooding figure with deep-set hazel eyes, sunk into himself over a small cup of tourkiko, the rich, black coffee of Greece. Although he was reserved when my husband introduced ourselves to him, he became friendlier when he learned that my husband had come expressly to Hydra to meet him. After that, we joined a group of five or six foreigners of which Leonard was a passive member. He sat amongst us, but always with an air of distraction.

After checking on our mail, if it had arrived on the unpredictable winter ferry, all the foreigners huddled together at the same waterfront tavern for morning coffee or a shot of ouzo. Afterwards we would either climb the worn steps up the hill away from the port, or thread our way around the hill to our small white rented house with its brilliant blue shutters. There we would spend the rest of the day painting, or writing, or walking the island as I did, my long black wool skirt tearing around my ankles in the wind, as I breathed in the cold fresh air of the Mediterranean winter.

I remember very vividly the day that Leonard asked me to go to the local cinema with him. I was surprised that he had done so because he had scarcely seemed to notice me all of those times that the three of us sat around a small, round table in the bare taverna with its wooden floor, the two men talking to my silence. We three seemed to accept as perfectly normal that Leonard had asked only me to accompany him that night. It was as though he was borrowing me from my husband, trying me out like a new suit of clothes to be returned to the shop keeper spotless and unwrinkled.

I had never been to that movie house, nor hardly believed that one existed, so I was excited, waiting for the night to come. I recall meeting Leonard at the port and together climbing the steep uneven stone stairs halfway to the top of the hillside. We reached a small building at the side of the staircase. It had a single room with a few rows of plastic chairs. A home projector noisily spat out a black and white film. We were the only people there.

Leonard took my hand as we sat side by side. My eyes were riveted to the screen. His intensity frightened me. I sensed his wanting something from me, but I did not know what. This made me feel stupid and very awkward. I felt I must be doing something wrong, or worse, that in a short amount of time, I would become offensive to him. I seemed to be hurting his feelings by not understanding what he wanted from me. At one point, he turned to me in the darkness and said, "You have a perfect nose." This seemed a strange comment, isolated as it was from anything that had passed between us. I sat stiffly, staring at the senseless screen and saying nothing in response.

Later, he walked me back through the hills in the interior of the island where I had never been before nor ever went again, although I see them so clearly in memory. We did not speak. The moon was full and lit the way down to the sea. The wind was strong but kind to us, and to the night. When we reached the door of the house where my husband was waiting for my return, Leonard said good-night and politely kissed me on the cheek before we parted.

* * *

I remember being with Leonard again in 1969, almost two years later, at the fabled Chelsea Hotel in Manhattan, then in its heyday as a stomping ground for many different sorts of creative artists. I do not remember how he knew that I was in the city and found me; or perhaps I found him. But

I vividly remember his characteristic courtly manner as he reached for my hand to help me out of the bouncy yellow cab I had taken downtown. I was in New York visiting a girlfriend, after returning from Mexico, to which I had travelled for a quick divorce.

I remember that I wore a black Fortuny pleated trouser set lent to me by the friend I was visiting. I had no money and certainly no clothes appropriate for New York occasions, largely because I had only my diminished European wardrobe which had been designed for travel or life on a Greek island. My long black hair, parted in the middle, fell in thick waves to my breasts where I had pinned a red rose that was nearly obscured by it.

I had taken that taxi, an extravagance I could ill afford, so that the lone flower would not be crushed in a crowded subway. Besides, I was excited to see Leonard in New York. By now, he had reached cult-like celebrity status. Rumor had it that he was no longer with Marianne, the woman with whom he had been living on Hydra and the woman immortalized in his song, "So Long, Marianne." We were two people unencumbered by ties to anyone. Somehow that mattered.

Leonard's voice was low, and his manner soft and gentle as he greeted me. Leading me into the hotel's lobby, he politely asked if I would like a drink or dinner. I was grateful for his attention, but I became distracted by the people passing us, all of whom called to him respectfully in greeting. It seemed a long time before he took me by the elbow and led me into the dining room. There he walked me from table to table introducing me to the other diners as though I were the celebrity they had been waiting for. "This is Beverly, folks," he said repeatedly. I was so intimidated that I could only nod dumbly in acknowledgment. To my relief we finally settled at our own table and I could turn my focus on him.

He seemed troubled. But then, he had always seemed so. I could sense my excitement diminish. This was the same Leonard, at thirty-seven, withdrawn and preoccupied, whom I had known on Hydra. For an instant he had looked directly at me, his hazel eyes like searchlights piercing the semi-darkness to find mine. Then the searching look was gone, withdrawing behind a wall of polite conversation about his latest recording, which had been made in his native Canada. His need to make a connection with me floated away into the dining room's smoky air.

Helplessly, I tried to draw him back, but I could not. I felt his loneliness. I felt my own. He had tried hard to dispel them both by extending his hand to me, flattering me and caring for me. It had not been enough. I had not been enough. It had not worked. Not there in the Chelsea Hotel nor on Hydra the previous winter.

I wish now that I had not thought then that he was sad; and that I had not felt his loneliness to be intimidating. I wish that I had warmly held the hand he extended to me. Pressing it, I would have turned to kiss him tenderly on the cheek and said, "You are a good man, Leonard. I see you. We will be friends forever."

But I said nothing. The evening ended uneventfully.

Months later, I began to feel that same sense of isolation that Leonard was presumably feeling back then. It stayed with me for years. I wanted to reach out to him, but I could not. He was too famous. I was too afraid that he would not remember that night on Hydra when the moon shone bright and the wind blew around us in balmy bursts. Nor did I want to remind him of his intense need to make a connection with another human being on that arid island in the Aegean or in that exciting atmosphere of the Chelsea Hotel. That need had been thwarted, at least by me. But I do believe that at some point in his lifetime the wanting must have been fulfilled—and expressed in that exquisite burst of "Hallelujah!" in his impassioned song of that name.

I cannot know how Leonard arrived at his Hallelujah moments, whether it was through his guru at the monastery in California where he lived for eight years, or maybe through his relationship with his children before his death in 2016 at the age of eighty-two. But I do believe that the sense of transcendence in some of his songs is directly related to his understanding, at last, of connectedness.

CHAPTER EIGHT:

MEETING HUSBAND

Altogether I had lived in England for nearly fifteen years, nine of which were largely taken up with hours spent lying on my first analyst's couch. To the right of the elegant, Georgian-style home where she kept her office, was the canal for which the neighborhood was named. I hardly registered the presence of the quietly flowing water, so eager was I to follow the long pathway that connected the broad quiet street where I had parked my old Morris Minor to her shiny black front door with the gold knocker. The house was deeply set back from the road and a distance from its next-door neighbor, making it seem an isolated and precious space waiting for me to inhabit it. How surprised I was to one day encounter my analyst's husband on the premises, shaking my sense that she existed within it, for me alone.

My office was only a five-minute drive away. I had moved on from my two previous jobs, the first in social services and the next, working for a non-profit agency, because I thought it important to broaden my experience by learning to work with children as well as adults. My third and final job in England was working as a therapist in a child guidance clinic in Kilburn, a part of London near the Tavistock Clinic, a training and research facility for psychotherapy and psychoanalysis in Hampstead, and also close to the home and clinic of Anna Freud, Sigmund Freud's daughter.

The area was saturated with therapists, therapists in training, therapists doing research, therapists writing books about their work, and therapists sharing work across the different clinical establishments. In fact, one of my workmates and sometime therapy partner, as we tended to work in pairs in the child guidance clinic, was Ireni Freud, the wife of Anna Freud's adopted son.

Three, sometimes four lunch hours, each week were spent lying on that couch. On the ride back to my office not only did I need to adjust my make-up and my mind to address the daily tasks at hand, I also needed to consume a quick lunch. Keeping my body together in those days was not easy, as the bulk of my meager earnings went to my analyst. Even though I had been given a reduced rate for "professionals working in the field," I had to eke out money for the odd drink at the pub or evening at the theater.

And although I've always loved nice clothes, buying clothes was also not in my budget. I managed to assuage my craving by sometimes going to the local Marks & Spencer, a signature department store on every high street in England, where good quality met somewhat frumpy style. And happily, the store had an easy return policy. I would "shop," bring items home, try them on in front of my wardrobe mirror, and hang them on the door until they were returned, unworn, a few days later. While I had these items, I could think them into my life and live out the fantasy that they were mine. I was the same person who as a child could slowly lick an ice cream cone, savoring it long after my brother had finished his.

But as the years went by and my analysis took root in me, I found myself missing my family back in the States more and more. With understanding myself, came increased love for them. These newly warm feelings resulted in my returning home for regular annual holiday visits. In turn, members of my family came to England to visit me. Our lives were connecting again. By 1985, after I'd been living abroad for nearly twenty years, I had thoughts of going home for good.

After my sister went off to college in the late 1970s, my mother left the suburbs to which she had moved after my father's death and her marriage to my stepfather, and went back to Morristown, the small town where she, my brother and I had been born. Morristown was the place my grandparents had emigrated to directly from Russia in the early 1900s, my brother had returned there to raise his family, and most of my relatives on both sides of my family still lived in that town. Legendary battles had been fought in Morristown during the Revolutionary War and maybe because of that, the place emanated a sense of both history and endurance.

Picturesque stone churches were dotted around the "green," a square space in the middle of town. There a person could sit on a bench amid the shrubs and the flowers in summer, and in winter under the evergreens ablaze with Christmas lights guarded by Nutcracker soldiers. Morristown felt to me a little like rural England with rolling countryside extending in every direction outward from the town. I was beginning to realize that Morristown felt like home.

By 1980, the visits to my mother that had been sporadic in the past, were becoming a regular yearly event. As my analysis continued and my disastrous relationships began to recede, I began to focus more on my relationship with my mother, a subject that I had given very little space to in my analytic sessions. I later realized that this was because I had thought there was nothing wrong with our relationship, while my current love relationships felt very wrong. Besides, my own mother was the only one that I had ever known. She hadn't been cruel to me, I reasoned, she had tried her best I kept saying, but as I began to bring her into the sessions, I was able to see how her depression had impacted my life. I do not remember feeling angry towards my mother, simply sad.

And then my own sadness emerged. What had I done with my life? Why had I thrown away my husband for a womanizing alcoholic? The divorce from my first husband, and the life I had known with him, was now feeling like a terrible loss. I missed him. I longed for him. Had our marriage really not felt right? Why had I not given it more time? I chastised myself for what now felt like an impulsive decision to divorce him.

It was out of this painful awareness of the life I had lost that I began to mourn the loss of my own father, thirty-five years earlier. And from the ashes of that deep and what seemed endless mourning rose the need to have a good man love me again and be caring of me and be true to me.

I realized two other things while lying on that couch in the Georgian house by the side of the canal. The first was that I wanted to be a wife, somebody's wife, and not just anybody's wife but an archetypal wife to a real husband. The second was that I did not want to be buried in England, on foreign soil. It seemed apparent that in order not to do the latter, which would likely happen if I married someone who was British, I needed to take radical action on the former. So I did. Abruptly.

In January of 1986 I gave notice at work, to my analyst, to the Guild of Psychotherapists, a psychotherapy training institute which I had only just begun attending, and to my very dear friends, and I left England later that month. I was forty-six years old. I had no job to slide into, no money, no friends left in America, no professional network, and just a single suitcase that I again brought to my mother's home, which was now a small one-bedroom apartment. My mother, happy that I was coming home, rewarded me by generously handing over her bedroom to me while she slept on the pullout sofa in the living room.

There I stayed for a year and a half until I acquired a job, a car, a few friends and an apartment of my own in my grandmother's disintegrating 150-year-old house that fronted on a six-foot square patch of yard. This small lawn, framed in hostas and hydrangea bushes and an uneven, slate sidewalk, separated the house from the busy main road that led into what had become the "bad" part of town. The third floor, where my grandmother had once housed immigrants from Russia, was empty and ghostlike. On the floor below that one, there was a vacant apartment that was to become mine.

My grandmother's friend, the widow Mary, had reared her son there but now that he was grown, they had left. I fled to that dwelling of transitional space like a migrating bird joining its flock from which it had become separated. This apartment seemed like a meeting point between my being an American but still feeling as if I were fresh off the boat.

The house was now also empty of my grandmother who, growing senile, had been dispatched to Florida to live with her youngest daughter. The ground floor apartment, where my grandmother had cared for her family, was now home to Martha, the person who had been her caretaker. She now lived there with her daughter and grandson. The four of us bonded together in that house which my uncle, the executor of my grandmother's estate, was managing.

The rent was high, the floors were creaky, the windows stuck, especially in the humid summer air, and there was no air conditioning or screens on the windows. But the warmth provided by the heating system in winter was ample as were the many beautiful pieces of antique furniture that had been left in place for Martha and me. I lovingly rearranged the furniture in a way that pleased me, feeling secure in what felt like my grandmother's presence.

* * *

While living in England, the only times that I realized how British I had become were when I had visitors from America. They would tease me about my use of such words as "jolly," and I would remind myself how British I had grown when they asked for ice for their drinks at the pub and I found myself cringing. "Small refrigerators churn out small amounts of ice," I wanted to say, but I left it for them to figure out, which they never did. Visitors were infrequent enough, however, for me to have forgotten that feeling of being a "foreigner" until I returned home permanently.

Then the feeling of being foreign became relentless. I was continually reminded of my accent as if living abroad for two decades would have not impressed anything on me. Because I was overwhelmed by the sheer size of supermarkets, I took to doing my shopping by buying whatever was at the ends of aisles. With one swift walk across the store latitudinally I could grab whatever was there, usually the sale items, and flee.

I was staggered by the enormous size of portions put on the plates in restaurants and by the way that these same plates were attacked without thought of elbows on table and napkins in laps. The cars were enormous as well and loose in their steering mechanisms, which made me think I would end up on somebody's manicured lawn with a touch of my fingernail. Voices were loud and children were so unchecked and abundantly present, that I found myself scowling and walking around tut-tutting to myself.

The number of items discarded also appalled me. Why use a paper cup when there is a glass one and it need not go into the waste heap? The abundance of food and sweets everywhere, especially at Christmas, made me think back to those more Spartan Christmases in England with nostalgia. Whenever the travel section of the Sunday New York Times featured an article about England, I read it and cried for the rest of the day.

America was not being good to me. In fact, apart from my family, it was not only indifferent to me but at times cruelly hostile. My British accent was a source of entertainment for most people I talked to, as well as suspect. As I had barely begun formal training to become a psychoanalyst, I was applying for jobs as a baseline social worker. Was it that my accented voice implied that I knew more than they did and, if so, was that reason to be rejected, and, if not, more reason still to reject me? I still don't know the answer to that question.

But I get ahead of my story. About two or three years before I left England in 1986, I experienced one of those self-conscious moments of being British without realizing that I was being British. My cousin Barbara on my father's side, came to visit me along with her husband.

The visit was unexpected. I had heard nothing of her for decades and knew only that her parents had recently died. As I sat waiting for them in the lobby of the Park Lane Hotel, an art deco extravaganza that faces Green Park and Buckingham Palace, where we had arranged by phone to meet, I saw a small pretty woman wearing very high heels hobble over to me with open arms and a warm and lovely smile. Here was my playmate from when I was three and four years old, my older cousin by four years who had lived a few doors away in a house similar to mine that our grandfather had built for us. Her father was my father's brother, and the two men had been business partners. Her mother was my mother's first cousin and our grandmothers had been sisters.

But no matter how close the blood bond had been, when my father died everything came apart. My grandfather's plan had been to form a conglomerate in the building trade, and with that in mind, he set up his sons in a paint and wallpaper business. But my grandfather died at fifty-six, only a few months before my father died at thirty-two. Out of the shambles we received a cash settlement and a few pieces of property.

My mother always angrily claimed that we had been cheated out of our fair share of the business. She hadn't known what she was doing, she said, adding that her relatives worked to confuse her even more. We didn't see them much after that. My mother was too angry, and my uncle too anxious about the whole thing, perhaps guilty as well, but we will never know. In any case, the result was that I felt I had lost the whole of my father's family, and when I saw Barbara again, I wanted to keep on seeing her. She was whatever I had left of him, and I was not going to lose him again.

That night we had dinner together, and she and her husband took me to the theater. The very last time I had seen them was at their wedding in 1958, 25 years earlier, where I was escorted by my mother's parents, my mother not having been invited. That night when the three of us met in London stands out vividly for me, and I write of it because that evening was like a golden moment out of time during the years I lived in England.

It was cold that night. Barbara bewailed the fact that she had left her furs back in America and I was thinking, "Bloody hell, furs? Plural?" Not feeling the cold in my own nondescript black cloth coat, I marveled at their life, so different from mine, so wonderfully frivolous and mundane. I wasn't envious or even jealous. I simply wondered what I was missing and, like the beautiful sweaters and skirts and coats from Marks & Spencer, I left the thought hanging from a peg somewhere in the wardrobe of my mind.

When I returned to the States in 1986, Barbara and I reconnected. I was busy looking for work and trying to stabilize myself in this new country that had become so unpredictable to me, so that when she said that she had a brother-in-law she wanted me to meet, I hardly paid attention. I had not remembered that her husband had a brother. Besides, his name, this brother-in-law's, was becoming a refrain, something floating around in the atmosphere without substance, as two years elapsed between the first of the many times Barbara told me about him and his actually phoning me to set up a date at the end of 1988. He later told me that he hadn't phoned because he did not trust her judgment when she told him that I would be "a breath of fresh air next to all of barracuda-like ladies" he had been dating. Meanwhile, I had been going out with other men. I was not waiting around for him.

Oh, but I was waiting for him! People say, "I knew as soon as I saw him that he was the one," but I never believed them until it happened to me. It was the weirdest sense of surety that I have ever experienced. That day, it was early December of 1988, I remember looking down on him from the top of the staircase before descending the rickety stairs to meet him in the front hall of my grandmother's house. All that I could see was that he stood tall and that he had a large head of brown hair but as I reached the bottom two steps and turned as if in slow motion to greet him, I knew.

He was forty-eight years old and handsome at six-foot-one, with brown eyes and a swarthy, healthy complexion; but it was his dignified demeanor, his gentleness, the sense that he was a "gentleman" that went beyond his fine looks. Having let himself into the house through the glass-paneled Victorian doors with the broken lock, he was collecting me for a dinner date. Looking into his face as I approached him, I could see that he had a startled, scared expression that he concealed as though hiding it within his beautiful, tightly buttoned three-piece tweed suit. It looked as if it had been sent directly from Harrods, the luxury London department store. I later learned it was a Ralph Lauren special that in retrospect made me feel tacky in my hastily pulled together discount-store purchases of black woolen skirt and fuchsia silk blouse.

But not that night. That night I was unruffled by what I was wearing. Nothing felt wrong that night, not even his constant chatter about himself. He had bought a new car that day, he told me as we were riding in it to Valentino's Italian Restaurant, a short distance away in the center of town. He talked about that transaction and about having moved to Morristown when he was eight years old: how he often passed my grandmother's house when he was a boy walking into town for an ice cream soda at the drugstore around the corner, and how he had loved Morristown and still did, but didn't get there much because of his busy pediatric practice in nearby Bergen County.

I listened. I knew that he was frightened and that he was talking as a cover for his fear. I even knew that at the end of the night when he was seated on my tiny couch and I, in one of my grandmother's chairs, and we were discussing if we would see each other again and he said he didn't know because he hadn't felt "chemistry" with me, I knew that he was talking nonsense, plain "scaredy-cat" nonsense.

113

The man had been married and divorced three times, and he had two sons in their twenties. Of course he would be scared of having a fourth wife. Besides, no man had ever not been attracted to me that I knew of. Hadn't I just been out the night before with a blind date, a nice man from England who had called me a "knockout" and begged me for a second date? At 5'2" and 120 pounds, fit and healthy, I felt that I looked not much different than when I was in my twenties, except happier, more relaxed. His matrimonial history combined with his reaction to our chemistry were interesting thoughts that I would ponder for the two months before he contacted me again. But my sense of knowing who this man was underneath his actions and words never wavered.

And when he did contact me, I got rid of the other two suitors I was dating and he got rid of his fear, or at least enough of it to relax into our getting to know each other. He was determined to get marriage "right," he later told me. And he did, brave man that he is. Brave to keep "pushing on the door," as the line goes in a gospel song I once heard about trying to make it into Heaven.

PART TWO:

BEHIND THE OPAQUE SCREEN: CASE HISTORIES AND THE PATIENT/ ANALYST RELATIONSHIP

As a man dismayed who turns to face the facts
changes his fear to trust in his own strength
when to his eyes the truth has been uncovered
So I changed; and when my leader saw me freed
From those anxieties, up by the rampart
he moved, and I behind him, toward the Height.
Dante (Purgatory)

What Dante, writing in the fourteenth century said, could also be said of psychoanalysis.

In the second part of this book, I describe several of my patients and trace both their growth, and implicitly, my own, as I try to guide them away from the constraints of their everyday anxieties toward what the legendary Medieval poet described as "the height." Having gone through my own psychoanalysis, I know the road well. I know what it feels like to be frightened of change. And I know that part of my fear involved thinking and feeling differently about people who, with the best of intentions had fed, sheltered, and cared for me, yet had in some crucial way deeply betrayed or disappointed me.

I know how frightening an unknown future can be. I know how necessary it is to risk going after that which a person needs and wants and how important it is to know that a person has just enough wholeness to be able to take such a risk, even if it should fail, as so often happens on the first try. And I know what freedom feels like when self-sabotage is no longer a habitual occurrence.

I am about to tell the stories of a few of the patients whom I have seen over the years, patients whose stories illustrate how therapy, whether we call it psychoanalytic, psychodynamic, or psychoanalytic psychotherapy—all therapies that aim to go deeply into the psyche—can triumph over behaviors that have trapped a person into living self-destructively. Such behaviors kill vitality and infect humanity because they destroy one's potential to grow, to create, to love. Even if these behaviors have lasted for decades, change, which may take years to accomplish, can be achieved.

The clinical stories range from a young, severely depressed mother who isolated herself from her husband, young children and the outside world when the life she had planned for herself imploded, to another young woman who was paralyzed by anxieties stemming from childhood sexual abuse, and yet another with a somewhat similar childhood history, who repeatedly chose unavailable partners.

Physical and mental childhood abuse was an underlying factor for two patients who were initially unable to put into words their traumatic experiences. One had perpetual and secretive fantasies of suicide that were played out in treatment until, after many years of therapy, she was free of them and leading the full and happy life she had always wished for. The other, who never spoke beyond the first session, was helped to go on with his young life after a year of being in treatment, as did another young person whose underlying rage was stultifying and caused her to be depressed until she felt she had been "listened to" and validated.

In writing these patients' stories, I reached out to them to ask permission for disclosure, even though names, genders, and other identifying information had been changed in order to preserve confidentiality. They graciously gave their consent, one of them even saying, "After all you have done for me...."

If, as I write this, I dare to feel a little like an archetypal "wise old woman," then so be it. This, then, is the second part of my journey, the one in which I, who followed, have taken the lead.

CHAPTER NINE:

NAVIGATING THE THERAPY MAZE

I was at a party in England attended by trendy sophisticated Londoners in the mid-1980s when I was asked what I did. I had only just started training to become an analyst, so it was rather bold of me to reply that I was a Jungian analyst when I was merely dreaming of becoming one. But I was feeling out of place in this exalted world and wanted to wedge my way in by suggesting that I belonged to a discipline that seemed "British."

The response was another question: "A union analyst?" I was baffled for a moment until I realized that not everyone knew of the celebrated Swiss psychoanalyst Carl Jung who had worked closely with Freud to help develop what eventually became known as psychoanalytic theory. And, of course, the word "Jungian" was easily mistaken for a word that sounded like "union."

I understood then that there is no obvious link between the analytic world and the outer "real" world, and that although the two blended so easily for me, most people were totally unaware of the concept of a psychoanalytic thinking. This realization left me feeling even more of an outsider at that very cool event. My white lie had backfired, compounding my feeling of aloneness, as did my being psychoanalyzed.

Given that there is no obvious connection between the "real" world and the inner world of psychotherapy, it is no wonder that finding the right therapist is usually a random event. My luck in finding two remarkable analysts was considerable. I know that most people aren't so lucky because they are not part of an analytic circle where they can get the feel of things from the outside before making a commitment to go through the psychoanalytic gate. When I started my analysis, I was working as a psychotherapist/social worker for a non-profit agency that had begun life as the Charity Organization Society. In those years, the mid-1970s, all of my colleagues were training to be analysts, and as a prerequisite to becoming an analyst, one must be analyzed one's self; I was in the perfect spot to find one.

So in 1985, toward the end of the time I was living in England, I thought it would be a good idea to develop a referral service along with a colleague at the child guidance clinic where we were working. It would short-circuit the process of finding an appropriate therapist for potential patients. The referral process would work like any matchmaking endeavor. By that point I had a pool of therapists whom I knew well along with prospective patients who would tell me what they were looking for in a therapist. We had brochures printed. The plan was ready to go. But as it turned out the timing was wrong. I had abruptly decided to return to live in the United States. There, I had to start my career all over again, and eventually, start, again, my training as an analyst.

But long before all of that, in 1976, I followed the suggestion of a colleague in London who referred me to my first analyst. My colleague was in training with the Society for Analytical Psychology, a training institute that combined Jungian ideas with the British School of Object Relations. As an undergraduate in college, I had been intrigued by the work of Carl Jung and combining parts of his theory with that of object relations made sense to me. The latter focuses on the mother-child relationship, particularly from infancy to early childhood when the infant takes in what, and how, the mother is providing for the baby's needs. This process, it is believed, becomes the foundation for individual personalities.

Even though I knew, intellectually, the theoretical backdrop for the way in which my first analyst and I were working, I was unaware that my words were going through any kind of theoretical sieve. Her well-timed interpretations seemed more mundane than academic, even though they derived from theory. This mix of the theoretical combined with skill, with intuition, and humanity is what, in my opinion makes for a good therapist no matter which kind of theory they follow. Some analysts who were great contributors to the school of British Object Relations were D. W. Winnicott, Ronald Fairbairn, Melanie Klein, Michael Balint and John Bowlby. After my first session with the woman whose name my colleague gave me, I knew that I needed to look no further.

In those years in the mid-seventies and for more than half of the nine years that I worked with her, my entire world became my analyst blotting out that other world, the one where people practiced the art of small talk. What became important to me was whatever transpired between the two of us, or whatever discoveries I was making about myself. I surrendered to the sheer luxury of having someone who was not only listening to me but seemed to love listening to me. I was mesmerized by the entire process, both of my benefitting from it and my clumsily trying to pass its benefits on to my clients.

Falling into this kind of psychoanalytic trance is not unlike falling in love. I found that I not only looked forward to every session, I could not wait to get there. I deeply admired my analyst, a gentle woman of about sixty whose gray eyes matched her hair, which was cut in a bob with a fringe across her forehead. She always wore thick woolen skirts and loose-fitting sweaters, and she seemed thoroughly English, which of course she was. Although somewhat frail-looking, she also had the air of having just come in from a rousing walk on the moors with her dogs (of which, in truth, she had none).

Our one common link was that we both had great-grandfathers who had been scribes. Mine, a Russian, copied the Bible by hand in his village in Lithuania and hers, an Englishman, wrote for the Queen in her palace. According to what she told me, he had been a member of the Queen's household, a high-ranking position indeed. I confess that I did not quite understand his position but so happy was I that we had family scribes in common that I dared not ask more about her relative. On her part, I am sure, she felt that she had already revealed quite enough about her background as in those days, analysts were supposed to reveal nothing at all about themselves.

And I had a deeper question. How could this woman be so interested in me and so understanding of my behavior, this clearly upper-class woman who seemed so calm and spoke so quietly? But it seemed so to me. As a result, I talked nonstop for that first year. I told her everything about the horrifying relationship I was having at the time with someone I had met at a disco. By then, my relationship with Jean Claude had dwindled to a correspondence between countries.

When I no longer could travel to Greece and could barely afford to pay my rent in England, he, in turn, was forced out of the house where he was living in the port in Symi because he could not cover the rent there. The beautiful wrought iron bedsteads, the colorful carpets from Turkey, all, he told me, he put in storage, only to tell me some time later that they had been stolen from storage, he didn't know how. In any event, they were gone, spirited off just as he and I were spirited away from each other.

I told my analyst all about the French painter, and also about my ex-husband, the writer. I spoke to her as if speaking to myself, but she listened, while I let my words float away in the air above my comfortably pillowed head. I lay on the green velvet couch, my eyes staring at the pale blank wall in front of me. She sat beside me on a large, winged armchair positioned a little behind my head. Sometimes when I twisted my head back to look at her, I would catch her with hers leaning against one wing of the chair in rapt concentration, her body looking small in that large container of an armchair.

In this way, sense was being made of my thirty-five-year-old life that was still causing me a great deal of pain. And thanks to this talking endlessly into the air above me with my analyst seated beside and a little behind me, I soon broke off that disco-yet-another-unsatisfying-relationship. Ridding myself of this entanglement felt like it had nothing to do with my analyst, nothing at all to do with anything I talked about with her. It seemed as if everything had happened spontaneously. I was only glad to "see the backside" of that relationship, as they say in England.

In the beginning, being with my analyst was like having a double, a doppelganger, but one who was detached from me so that she was free to pick me up when I fell and comfort me when I cried. I didn't ask for any of that; I couldn't have asked her for anything outright, being so in awe of her. But there was no need to ask anything as she instinctively knew, or so it seemed to me, when I needed help and when to keep out of things. She was her own person at the same time that she was so caring of me. No wonder I felt so comfortable on her sofa.

As I write this several decades later looking back on those days, I can see that what was going on was the ideal experience of being an infant and having a good mother. But back then, the experience simply felt comforting. With my analyst, I belonged. I was cared for and safe. Eventually, I would be able to carry these feelings with me into the outer world, although that was many years in coming.

* * *

It was while working with my first analyst that I became even more determined to be a psychoanalyst like she was–kind, compassionate and smart. But it wasn't until I had returned to the States and had lived here for ten years, that I found an institute that felt compatible to me. By then I was married for the second time and had my own private psychotherapy practice, having worked my way up from being a supervisor in the Family Service Agency while moonlighting at the Janet Woititz Clinic for Adult Children of Alcoholics.

So I began my institute training in 2001 at the New York Institute for Psychoanalytic Self Psychology. Institutes are organizations that must be approved by state education departments and exist to train psychoanalysts to work in a particular theoretical approach. Some have a separate program to train therapists in analytic thinking (psychoanalytic psychotherapists) with slightly less stringent requirements for certification. There are numerous differing theories, but the training in each institute is basically the same as the one I undertook.

Coursework, usually a minimum of four years of evening classes, is combined with clinical practice. Each training analyst must have two separate "control" patients and must be supervised by two different supervisors. In addition, each training analyst is required to be in their own psychoanalysis. The latter requirement is unlike any other training for therapists including that of psychologists. Although psychologists usually have doctorate degrees, and institute training gives no such title, psychologists, in my experience, rarely have been in their own therapy.

Psychoanalytic training is emotionally, financially, and physically costly, requiring a deep commitment to one's self, one's patients and to the profession. We analysts need to, at the least, know our own "disease," so that we are in a better position to cure those of our patients. Becoming an analyst is unlike becoming a medical doctor who doesn't need to have the disease in order to treat it.

Most analysts and psychoanalytic psychotherapists continue to remain a member of the institute where they received their training. There is usually a referral service existing within institute training organizations, but their pool of therapists is limited to members of their own institute. Referrals are made both to seasoned analysts and to those who are in training.

Candidates, the students in training, need "control patients" who will be seen three times a week, preferably lying on the couch, and be committed to long-term treatment. Low fees are therefore generally negotiated when referrals are made to therapists in training. The patient benefits by not only getting a very low fee, but also by having his analyst in training undergo supervision to ensure that the treatment goes as it should. Otherwise, finding a therapist is generally a matter of knowing someone who knows of someone. Whether or not it might be a good fit can feel like an afterthought.

One word more about finding the right therapist. There is something called "supportive work" in the field of mental health. It holds a very important place in therapy, but it is meant to be only a part, or sometimes a phase, of treatment. It does not disturb the psyche at a level that needs to be disturbed in order for permanent change to take place, but it can help the patient to "get back on his feet" again.

There is a pitfall in supportive work, however. Well-intentioned therapists, particularly those who have not had their own therapy, who offer support and "like" the patient, are not always able to step back far enough from the patient to effectively treat that patient, who then leaves therapy thinking that all is well despite the fact that nothing has really changed. The real danger is that unsuspecting patients who are feeling liked and supported are being cheated from getting a chance to understand and feel better about themselves.

* * *

My experience with my second analyst ten years later when I was back in the States, was very different from my first analysis. After more than nine years of lying on the couch in London from 1977 to 1986, I thought I'd had quite enough of analysis. But as I went into training in 2001 and it was required that I be analyzed by someone with the same theoretical approach as the institute at which I was studying, I had to commit to, at the least, an abbreviated version. This version turned out to be eight more years of lying on a couch, but this time it was a once-a-week basis as opposed to four times a week.

I chose a male analyst who was also the founder of the New York Institute for Psychoanalytic Self Psychology located on the Upper West Side of Manhattan, where the theories of Heinz Kohut, an Austrian psychoanalyst, are taught with an emphasis on the concept of "empathic attunement."

Discovered in the 1950's by Kohut in his work with his patients, empathic attunement operates by getting into another's experience, into "the shoes of another." The technique can be described as a gentle penetration of the analyst's mind into that of her patient, a penetration that creates a fusion as intimate as any physical intimacy. It is the meeting of two minds in order to understand an experience that is being blocked or has been repressed or avoided. The self in need of protection does not want to put a name to the feeling because to name it would cause some unknown imagined harm to ensue.

Here, the word, empathy, means getting into the experience of the patient in order to understand their inner world and to work from within it to affect change. It works. It does affect change, especially for repetitious, self-destructive behavior that has gotten in the way of our functioning. I was back to where I had started from, New York and navel-gazing intellectuals, but this time I was not just talking about psychoanalysis, I was going through that experience.

I am basically a very loyal person and it was hard for me to transfer my affection for my past analyst, even though nearly ten years had passed between the two experiences. In that time, I had remarried, acquired two stepsons in their twenties, and kept on working as a social worker therapist and as a private practitioner. I suppose, as a result, I was a bit oppositional with this new analyst. I liked where I was in my life and felt that I need ask for no more.

For starters, I did not want to lie on his couch which is the accepted, traditional practice in psychoanalysis, preferring to sit opposite him in a straight-backed, wooden armchair that was offered as an alternative. However, with his first good interpretation, I took him up on the offer he had made many times and slid from the chair onto his very uncomfortable analytic bed, placed against one wall of the rather drab consulting room. The pillow was thin as was the cot-like mattress that felt hard on my back.

And similarly, this analytic experience was a more ascetic one. It involved no cradling as the last one had. In fact, at those times when I could not stop myself from crying, I felt his impatience and did my best to get hold of myself. Or perhaps it was I who felt that I shouldn't be crying as I had had enough of that in my first analytic experience? I shall never know.

But despite my resistance, through him I gained further understanding of myself that I am now deeply grateful for. By "getting into my experience," as the "self psychologists" the Kohutians are called do, this analyst gave me back experiences that I could not define, that I was not consciously aware of, that had become so much a part of me that they weighed me down unknowingly. I can hear his deep, clear, actor's voice even now; with his shock of snow white hair, he seemed like the oracle of psychoanalysis, or simply the archetypal "wise old man."

For example, in a session in which I had been talking about a bimonthly visit to my mother, a fifty minute harrowing car ride from Bergen County where I was living with my second husband, he observed that I was treated "as a guest in my mother's home." As soon as he made that comment, I realized its truth. As I elaborated on his statement, I also realized that visits to my mother's home left me feeling that I had worked very hard to keep her happy and entertained. Afterwards I invariably returned from them feeling exhausted and dissatisfied.

The analyst had picked up on my feelings surrounding the encounters. He did this being attuned to my experience, "getting into my shoes" while I was not conscious of it. And by his doing so, pieces of myself were being given back to me that I had unthinkingly given away because I didn't recognize that I had them. Without him, I would have forever dismissed the visits as soon as they were over and gone about my business until the next unsatisfactory visit, repeating the pattern endlessly, mindlessly riding that exhausting hamster's wheel. Instead, I learned from a debilitating situation how to correct it simply by being aware of the reality of my own experience.

I loved my mother, in spite of her shortcomings with me. I wanted to see her. But through my second analysis I also learned how to stop working so hard to entertain her for the reward of a smile that didn't often come. My mother's expectations hadn't changed but mine had. It was not that I was inadequate because I couldn't help her. It was that my mother had unrealistic expectations of what I could provide for her. It was, to a lesser degree, like that death scene with my stepfather, when he returned home dangerously ill and was left in my care, along with my baby sister cradled in my arms. I could no more keep him from death than I could lift my mother's lifelong depression from her.

On further reflection, I was also able to connect these visits with a dream I'd had when I was five years old, a dream I've never forgotten. I remember, too, that the dream kept me awake for the rest of that night so long ago. I'd tried to interpret it in my first analysis, but it had always alluded me.

Here it is: I was walking down an alleyway holding a stick that I knew I needed, but only because it was mine. I was walking towards my mother, whom I could see in the far distance, calling to me from the wide doorway of a barn. The wind was blowing her long full skirt around her calves, and her dark hair was coiffed the way that ladies wore their hair in the '40s with a roll of hair pulled away from her face and tucked up around the back of her head. Her usually sculpted features were unclear except for her dark eyes sunken into grey hollows. Still she looked very soft and beautiful and helpless.

Then three monkeys approached me. They were "Hear No Evil, Speak No Evil and See No Evil" like the little statue kept in the curio cabinet in my grandmother's dining room. They had fascinated me, and one day when I had asked my grandmother about them, she explained who they were.

Here they were again in my dream asking for the stick, which I needed, which I wanted for myself, which I somehow knew was a part of me. I didn't want to let it go, but I also knew that if I wished to keep advancing forward to meet my mother, I had to surrender it. And so I gave the stick to the monkeys and kept on walking towards my mother as if I were walking against a strong wind. Suddenly I heard a gunshot ring out behind me. Frozen in my tracks, I stopped and watched as my mother fell to the ground, her skirts swirling round her, enveloping and burying her.

I realized in this, my second analysis that I was giving up a part of myself to my mother, that from the onset of this dream that I had at the age of five, I was giving away my birthright (the stick) in order to reach her, sensing that she was in trouble. But since I had only been a child, I failed to help her. My attempt had felt like hard work to me; I was walking against the wind, and still my mother was shot down dead.

So when I grew up and married for the first time at age twenty-two in 1963, I wandered away from my mother to find my own happiness. But not consciously knowing anything of my motivation, I looked for happiness in the wrong places. I was in need of a loving gaze but it was my mother's loving gaze I had needed, not the one of the French painter, an alcoholic older man who made a habit of indiscriminately giving loving gazes to women.

It saddened me, this second analysis, in the way that closing a coffin lid over a corpse is invariably sad. There is nothing more to be done. The past is understood and connected to the present in a way that makes the past obsolete. But I also felt liberated. I did not stop my visits to my mother, but because I became aware of what I was feeling and what they were doing to me, I was far less adversely affected by them.

I learned that this self-psychology analyst I had chosen was often, and surprisingly, on the mark, so I again fell into a psychoanalytic trance, if only partially. Parking in New York was a pain, driving there from New Jersey was no less stressful, but I wanted to know what self psychology was all about from a horizontal position. And I did, much to my benefit.

* * *

It is as if finding a therapist, whether she be a psychoanalyst or not, mirrors the accident of birth. We land somewhere without the option of choice. Like a parent, the therapist has the upper hand. He can abandon the patient or pretend to love when he just doesn't feel it, or love overmuch if his boundary issues are poor. The patient, like the child, is usually too dependent, too needy to be able to escape the situation if there is a sense that the match is not comfortable. Generally people are at their lowest point when they come into treatment. They arrive as though out of breath with the effort it took to get themselves there. They may not have the energy to move on if something about the analyst or therapist doesn't seem right to them. Then again, if something feels wrong, they think it has to be them. Didn't they need help in the first place?

CHAPTER TEN:

SORROW IN SUNLIGHT:
A FEW WORDS ABOUT DEPRESSION

We all know something of depression, that state of unhappiness, of despondency, of misery and melancholy. If we have not experienced a severe bout of it ourselves, we have from time to time felt its milder presence. That sense that nothing can excite, that what seemed so positive has turned into a negative, that feeling of being unlovable and of caring less for something we had once loved, has visited us all.

Depression manifests itself in various ways and latches onto people in varying degrees. And not surprisingly, there are manifold theories about how it operates. Some maintain that depression is chemically based and others that depression is caused by emotion alone. More recently, still other theories have emerged, notably, that it is the interaction between mind and body that determines how we feel. In the past half century, the field of neurobiology has made important contributions to our understanding as to how the brain and the rest of the nervous system function—an understanding that has transformed the field of psychotherapy in profound ways and dramatically shaped our understanding of how depression works.

Of particular importance to us as clinicians has been the research on memory. Neurobiologists speak of the formation of circuits or pathways formed in the brain through the repetition of activities. Such research has a great deal to teach us about both depression and addictive behavior. If a person gets depressed again and again, the relevant pathways in the brain will become deeper and deeper, making it harder to reverse the feelings.

In recent decades, medications have been developed to treat moderate depression. In addition, a host of other techniques, such as electric shock therapy (which is being used less frequently in the present) and more recently, ketamine treatments have been used to dispel depression. It is my general belief as a psychoanalyst that medication can take the edge off depression so that psychotherapy can begin. For many patients pharmaceuticals should be used only as a temporary measure to help understand depression's meaning for that particular patient, so the patient himself gains control over the emotion and through that understanding, banish depression for good. For others, ongoing psychopharmacological management may be needed.

There is a song that Billie Holiday sings that describes depression so accurately for me. In the song, titled, *Good Morning, Heartache*, she croons, "Good morning, heartache, you old gloomy sight . . . Good morning, heartache, sit down." Those awful feelings of gloom and despair, of fear and self-loathing that lead to depression are described in a resigned and not unfriendly, almost welcoming manner. She invites the inevitable into her room, as though heartache were a friend who would keep her company in her loneliness. Depression, misery, gloom—all are words for that friend who will always be there when no one else can, or will, show up. When misery is present, there is no room for anything else, especially other feelings. Any sort of brightness feels unbearable, particularly the cheerfulness of other people.

And as much as we loathe feeling miserable, misery can provide a temporary answer to intolerable thoughts and feelings. It brings with it "good" feelings, feelings of safety, because nothing and no one is allowed in, and feelings of familiarity, because once we have experienced depression, we know so well what it is and where we are. Knowing where we are seems preferable to having problems that seem to have no answers and feelings that seem to be unendurable. Misery brings comfort in the form of a darkened room containing a bed that feels soft, embracing and peaceful.

In the beginning, depression masquerades as a friend, albeit still an unwelcome guest, and for a time it seems to be a best friend, but it is not to be trusted. Misery, which is another name for depression, holds in its pocket keys to a prison cell. It is a possessive partner who arrives promptly at your door once you show a need for it, and refuses to let go despite your protestations. But who cares about the consequences, or even knows what they are, when a person is pushing rage aside so that it doesn't overpower him? Or when someone doesn't know how to take the next step in a crisis or even what the next step should be? Or when loss feels so overwhelming that the idea of continuing with life feels intolerable and the idea of taking one's own life increasingly attractive?

My purpose in writing about depression is to offer a slightly different perspective on understanding and treating it in order to make the condition more malleable and therefore more manageable. Acknowledging the importance of the presence of depression is the first step toward fighting it. Next comes understanding what lies beneath the depression followed by techniques designed to help ease it or make it disappear entirely. Misery can be very helpful as a comfort and as a form of temporary protection, but the stronger it is and the longer it lasts, the harder it is to escape its clutches. That is because depression can become an addictive state of the self. As with any form of addiction, repetition can breed enslavement to it.

* * *

My patient, whom I shall call Jaymie, was twenty years old when I met her and twenty-one when she left treatment in 2017. Depression is caused by many different circumstances, and for Jaymie it was caused by rage that could find no relief even when she expressed it. It is said that a lot of depression exists because it throws a cover over unacknowledged anger and therefore acts as a protectant. For Jaymie, who was articulate about her anger, it remained with her because the emotion hadn't been validated by others, nor had she examined it. Depression overtook her when there was no one else around to be the target of her anger.

Jaymie was a tall, dark-haired, lanky young woman; her pretty face was usually distorted by rage. She always looked unkempt, as if she had just tumbled out of bed and had not had time to comb her hair or brush her teeth before arriving at our sessions, usually late. Initially she made it obvious that she did not want to be in my office and was coming only because her mother insisted that she see a therapist.

Nor, to be honest, did I look forward to her visits. She angrily complained about all the people in her life, few as they were. Her negativity extended everywhere except towards her father, whom she spoke of hardly at all. But mostly, I felt uncomfortable because she expressed her rage at such a high volume, practically screaming at me. I was afraid that she could be heard out in the parking lot and through the walls of my office into the offices of other therapists in my building. At other times, I was afraid that these same eavesdroppers would want me to shut her up and simply make her do what she was supposed to do, like clean herself up or return to college or get a job.

Part of her ranting was about just that. Her mother and her older sister were constantly telling her to go back to school, to clean up her apartment, to go out and see friends. They were unable to connect with the feelings Jaymie wished to tell them about. Jaymie would, in turn, counter-attack and say that they were not doing what they should be doing either. Her older sister, she contended, should be settling the estate of their father, who had died of a heart attack two years earlier, as she had been made executor of his estate. And her mother should come to Jaymie's apartment to help her clean it up.

Jaymie resented any time spent away from her apartment. She delayed grocery shopping until the cupboards were bare, and she ordered take-out whenever she remembered to eat. She now lived alone, her boyfriend having recently left her. Described as a dumb loser, the fellow could do nothing right in Jaymie's eyes. He was helpless, she told me and couldn't even help her keep the apartment in good repair. He was always anxious, a "stupid" student, and a momma's boy. In fact, his mother materialized one day to bring him back home. Still, the boyfriend had been all that Jaymie had.

Jaymie had dropped out of college when her father died. Her parents had divorced when she was ten years old, after which her mother moved out of the neighborhood where they lived, leaving her in the care of her father. Her sister, who by then finished college, was able to go out on her own, and had become professionally successful. As the executor of their father's estate, this state of affairs only exacerbated what had already been a toxic relationship between the two.

At the time Jaymie was referred to me by her mother, who had moved back to be near her daughter in an effort to help her. Jaymie wanted her mother's help, but it never seemed enough, and her mother's efforts always ended in Jaymie criticizing her and becoming even more angry. All that Jaymie wanted, she repeatedly said, was to get her share of her father's estate and to be left alone so that she could remain in bed all day with her large cat sleeping beside her, the two of them surrounded by myriad empty cartons that had contained takeout food that she hadn't bothered to throw away.

Jaymie did not know, at a conscious level, that what she really wanted was to be listened to and understood. I knew that what was required of me was to listen to her rage-filled ranting, to try to understand her unending anger and to validate her feelings. Otherwise, my presence, too, would not be needed.

Through session after session, Jaymie raged about the people in her life, angrily describing how they had either let her down or abandoned her. When her beloved father had done so by dying suddenly and unexpectedly, her entire world collapsed. I could easily empathize with her rage. She had been let down. She had been abandoned. Even her sister who would promise to meet her at the bank to give her money, cancelled or arrived just as the bank was closing. What else was left for Jaymie except her bed, her cat, and oh, yes, marijuana? It had taken six months for Jaymie to let me know that she was self-medicating with marijuana, if and when she could get it.

As Jaymie felt more and more validated, she began to talk about her parents and their difficult relationship and was able to express some anger towards her father, who formerly had been above reproach in her life. She talked of college and regretted having dropped out, although she did not feel quite up to returning as yet. She became more forgiving of her sister's faults as the estate slowly got sorted out. She frequently spoke of wanting to move out West, where marijuana was legal and easier to get and where she could be on her own. She began researching living accommodations there and mapping out a motor trip.

Although I had interpreted Jaymie's use of marijuana as a crutch to relieve her emotional pain and she accepted that explanation, she was not willing to let go of this need. Nonetheless, she became energized so as to help herself have a future, to bring some change into her life, and to get out into the world to experience it. She was beginning to calm down. I found myself looking forward to our sessions as I observed the emergence of the fine young woman who had been locked within her own rage.

Our work together had expanded her horizon, I told myself. More important, she was beginning to make sense of her anger, which previously had held her back, keeping her stuck in her misery. At this point in treatment, off she went. She had set a departure date for her trip, and when it arrived, she followed through on her plan.

About a year after Jaymie left the area, I received a phone call from her to confirm that I had gotten all the money she owed me and to thank me for all of the help I had given her. I was, I must admit, happily surprised to receive such gratitude from her and, to learn that she was doing all right. I was glad to hear a positive note in her voice.

* * *

Anna was another patient who suffered from depression but of a severe, clinical kind that is called major depressive disorder. When Anna's husband brought her to me for help about two decades ago, she was staying in bed all day and was sapped of the energy to do anything else except lie there. "Make her better," he implored me.

The husband had approached me in the spring of 2002, six months after the terrorist attack on the World Trade Center. Anna came to my office under duress and would speak of nothing except the tragedy of 9/11, saying that while it had been upsetting to her, she was in no need of help. Although I discovered that she had no direct connection to the attack, apart from that of geography as she lived across the river from the explosion, she kept it in the forefront of our sessions so that she could hide from me what she really felt and what was really happening to her.

A pretty, petite, thirty-two-year-old woman, the mother of five, Anna had been born in 1965 in the United States to newly arrived immigrants from Croatia. Her husband was also Croatian. They met almost as soon as he arrived in the States in 1982 and were married when they were eighteen and twenty years old, respectively.

Her husband had done well in this country. He quickly enjoyed prosperity, and the lifestyle of Anna and her young children brought her much joy. Then out of the blue, it seemed, she refused to leave her bedroom and kept to her bed. When the children tried to enter, she discouraged them. Their grandmother, who lived next door, took over their care.

In the beginning of our work together, there were times when Anna's husband could not pry her out of bed to bring her to my office. Weeks went by in this way. But, gradually as our sessions continued, Anna began to trust me, an outsider with no connection to her immediate family and her large extended family who lived nearby.

Bit by bit, her story unfolded, and together we came to understand that the implosion of the Twin Towers, the devastating event that many people had literally watched as it happened, was a metaphor for her own private world. Her husband's business had miserably failed, leaving the family with lawsuits and no money. A bright woman with no confidence in herself, Anna did not know what to do. She opted out of this seemingly unsolvable dilemma by unconsciously protecting herself with depression. Miserable as it made her, as unhappy as she was in her depressive state, that emotion provided a thick-walled prison cell where she felt safe from hostile intrusions.

Gradually, through our work together, it was revealed that Anna had had a history of things precious to her being taken away.

Since her childhood, she had been forced to relinquish any good that came her way because of an older brother who was both jealous and suffered from bipolar disorder and whom the entire family submitted to because of his uncontrollable rage. We learned, much later in treatment when Anna, herself, was putting together the pieces of her past, that Anna's early and good relationship with her mother had ended when Anna started kindergarten. There was no longer time for mother and daughter to be alone together, no time when Anna's mother could freely give of her love to her.

The behavior of her older brother dictated that he was to be the center of his mother's attention and the family submitted to his demands. Because her brother was not himself married, he would not allow his family to indulge his sister, and as a result her wedding celebration had to be reduced from its original splendor. Even the wedding dress that Anna had happily chosen for herself had to be returned because her brother insisted that she have a lesser one, one that he had control over.

After her marriage and up until the attacks of 9/11, safety had meant keeping herself and her children at home together, keeping them as far away from her brother as she could and not even allowing herself to have friends because of her fear that they, too, would be taken away. Clearly talking to a stranger therapist about her fears was taking a huge risk that, at an unconscious level, took time for both of us to understand.

My work with Anna revealed how difficult it is for a person to move out of depression, and how easy it is to move back into it. As Anna talked about her fears, her disappointments, her inner world and her childhood, her depression lessened. Eventually she was able to leave her home to go out to work every day. That was a huge milestone for someone who had not been out to work since she was seventeen years old.

Despite all of the nineteen years of our on-again-off-again work together, there were times when she still had to fight the urge to retreat to her bed, to stay there and shut out the world. A reminder of something from the past that still disturbs her would take her back to her bedroom again, as if a trigger had been pulled. We worked to discover what that catalyst was and how the present differed from the time when she was unable to control the past.

Today these episodes of feeling depressed come less and less frequently, and they are over more and more quickly. We both feel that Anna has much better control over her life, a life that has become transformed with therapy. It has taken years for these changes to happen, but they have come, and they are certain and long-lasting.

* * *

As much as transformation is wished for and dreamed about, it is frightening because of its unfamiliarity and the fears that unfamiliarity bring. Will I lose what I already have? Can I risk holding onto the good when I get it? Will it be taken from me again, and so what is the use in having it to begin with? These are the silent questions that come with change, for Anna as well as for countless others.

The pull to return to the prison cell where life stagnates speaks to the difficulty of all psychological change. We fear what we want, especially when we get a taste of it, and so we return to what we have known. If it was difficult to cut into the repetitive, self-destructive behavior, it becomes even harder to stay with life as we had always wished to live it.

When this new air has begun to be breathed, therapy enters a new phase. Therapy becomes a process of "working through," a repetition of the "good" replacing the "bad," the old, the familiar. Like a car that has got stuck in the mud and needs to be rocked in a forward and backward motion until it makes its way out onto dry road again, so goes treatment at this point. And this part of treatment can last for a very long time, until new habits are formed, new brain imprints made, the old ones disintegrated with lack of use. Then we are able to live without the fears that had kept us from having the life we had only wished for.

Anna has been remaking her life through therapy. Eventually her depression should disappear altogether. This will happen when the world that she has longed for, a world in which she feels free, becomes her new reality, and the old one just, a memory. Billie Holiday didn't make it. Anna, I feel certain, will.

CHAPTER ELEVEN:

SILENT AND SPEECHLESS IN THERAPY

Has an analyst, or any therapist, the right to drop a patient if that patient proves too difficult, too needy for that particular analyst? Does it say anywhere that once a patient comes through your door, you are obliged to work with that patient, no matter what symptoms the patient is presenting or how they're being presented? As analysts, we know that we may have blind spots and thus there are some patients we cannot help. And as much as analysts might not want to admit it, we also come across patients for whom we feel antipathy. We simply do not want to work with them. It is appropriate to refer those patients to another therapist. If the patient does not want to be transferred, there are other less obvious ways to address the issue, such as raising the fee.

But nowhere does it say that a therapist must work with a suicidal patient, or an addict, who reveals himself well past entering through our gate. That gate is never a straight-forward one. We often do not know what ghosts have entered the room along with the patient until that patient is comfortably seated (metaphorically) in our presence. It is at that point that an explosion can erupt. After working for months to develop trust in the relationship, all is revealed. Or as Freud would say "the layers of the onion" have been peeled to nearer the core. We, as therapists, then face ourselves. "Can I work with this patient? Can I endure it?" As with the marital vow "in sickness and in health," we either assume the obligation that is implied in the vow or opt for a divorce.

I have found that there are certain analysts who attract patients who are difficult; and others whose patients arrive at their door ready to work. The latter fit exactly into Freud's "talking cure." They are aware of their problems and want to grow out of them. But many of my patients are unable to put their thoughts and feelings into speech. While in training to be an analyst, I once complained to my supervisor that I was receiving patients whom other therapists seemed not to have. I was working with a highly suicidal patient at the time and others, who if not suicidal, were at high risk. "They would not be with you," he said, "If they did not sense that you could work with them."

I remember one young man who came to me early on in my career, before I had started my psychoanalytic training in this country. The year was 1986. I had returned to America from England and had difficulty finding work. I applied for many jobs, made myriad phone calls every day regarding work possibilities, and became accustomed to my phone messages being ignored, or receiving negative feedback from job interviews if I received any response at all.

Finally, much to my relief and surprise, I was hired as a social work supervisor, a position I had not even applied for. The advertisement clearly asked for a beginning social worker, but the woman who interviewed me thought that I should be in a higher position, had one available, and gave it to me. It was a good fit in all ways. I was working in a Family Service Agency during the day and began moonlighting in the evenings trying to get a private practice going. I don't remember how this particular patient found me, but my office in Morristown where I was also living, was in the vicinity of where he was living, and he probably saw my sign as he passed by my door.

He was the most solitary individual I have ever met. He was about twenty years old, tall and lanky, and with a very flat affect. This meant, in his case, that there was no emotion attached to the horrific events he was telling me about. He spoke only in the first session. With head bowed, he told me that his father had beaten and abused him throughout his childhood. At age fourteen he had moved next door to live with a neighbor. He continued to go to school and walked past his father's front door daily, behind which the rest of his family continued to live.

After that brief description of his background, he spoke not again in all of our sessions. He always arrived at my office exactly on time and left on time without my ever having to announce the session's end. He never even said hello or good-bye. Nothing. In desperation, I spoke to a psychiatrist about him, hoping to get some advice as to how to proceed. He told me to tell this young man to leave therapy because in order to make use of it, speech was necessary. I felt somehow that that was wrong and because of that, I couldn't follow the advice. So I clumsily soldiered on, not knowing what else to do. I remember feeling that it was my problem and not his that we were unable to do "talk therapy." He had come for help. I had to figure out how best to give it.

Throughout many sessions, we sat in silence, he and I. Whatever few words I ventured to say to him were met with silence, as though I were speaking into a blank space. It was as if he were trying to make himself as small as possible so that I would not notice him. If I didn't notice him, then I couldn't hurt him.

I was not able to verbalize this reaction at the time because I was too inexperienced. I only knew that he and I must somehow be put at our ease with each other. On a whim, I brought books of fairy tales to the session and read to him. He seemed to like this. I felt that it was soothing for him. It was certainly calming for me. I did know that underneath his silence, he was full of rage and shame. He needed someone to just be there with him, maybe if only to prove to himself that he had some control over his rage, that he wasn't going to kill anyone with it, perhaps even me.

Our sessions ended after about a year because I had moved my office to a different town that was about an hour away from where he lived. Travelling an hour to get therapy is a long way for anyone, but for this young man, who had stayed so close to home for virtually his entire life, it must have seemed like travelling to the moon. I gave him my new address and urged him to continue therapy, but he opted not to.

About two years later, he rang me to say that he had a girlfriend and was planning to marry her and could he come back for a few sessions. I was very happy to hear from him and eagerly gave him an appointment with exact directions for getting to me, but he could not find me. He phoned to say that he was lost. I tried to direct him again. Again he tried to find me, but he could not and phoned to tell me so. I have heard nothing from him since.

As a seasoned therapist, I am not proud of myself for reading him those books. I should have stayed with the silence and tried to figure out where his was coming from. That would have been the so-called empathic stance described by the Austrian psychoanalyst Heinz Kohut best known for his development of self psychology. But I am certain that I knew intuitively that this patient needed me to be there in any capacity. I could have stood on my head throughout the session as long as I did not intrude upon his space, which he so jealously guarded and carefully protected.

At the time, I suppose I was not brave enough to be without a prop, without something placed between us. But at least I was there, and that alone seemed to help him to move on. Was that therapy? Absolutely, although I did not think so then. I remember feeling guilty about what I had done. I had broken the rules as I had been taught. I kept this guilty secret to myself for years. It was not until I started my institute training in self psychology that I realized that I had been intuitively empathic with that young man. In his case, it was the empathy that counted.

* * *

Other patients come for help because they have symptoms that make them uncomfortable. They want relief, and they want it quickly. They do not want to know that the symptom is there because there is an underlying problem. They only want to know how to get rid of it. To the analyst, these could be termed "resistant" patients, however, there are many forms of therapy in which symptom relief is the goal.

One such approach is called Behavior Modification Theory. It can be successful in helping a patient change his own negative behavior which in turn changes the environment's responses to him, and because of that, he may be able to move forward with his life. But he will not be encouraged to ask why he behaves in a certain way and come to understand himself at a deeper level. My feeling is that he will find himself uncomfortable again with another kind of behavior that is self-defeating, and that even in this new territory, he will stop there and be stuck. But Behavior Modification Therapy does have its uses, and I have referred people to therapists who work in this way.

Psychoanalysis is the opposite of behavioral modification therapy in that it takes a long time for change to occur. This is so because psychoanalysis involves burrowing deeply into the psyche. It moves the ocean floor that underlies the waves—no small feat. Psychoanalysis aims at self-understanding, which is designed to lead to symptom relief. Once the patient recognizes why the symptom is there and what use it has, that symptom no longer has the same energy. It is then possible not only to take charge of the symptom, but also the situation that created it. One's very structure has changed. A new configuration can be formed.

When one patient, whom I shall name Claire, came for therapy with the goal of wanting, as she put it, "to have more fun" in her life, I had not yet learned that there are some patients who come with secrets that underlie the seemingly benign intent. The year was 1994. By this time, I had stopped working for the family service agency and had started a private practice, and I was soon to begin my psychoanalytic training in New York.

In those first few sessions I took my patient's intentions literally. She was a hardworking woman with two children and a husband whose idea of fun, she told me, was being glued to the TV watching sports. But, she quickly added, "No complaints. He is a good guy." It was more that her children had provided the joy in her life and they were leaving home for college. She knew she needed to do something to remedy her situation. To me this sounded like a good reason to come into therapy.

But as the months went by and I heard the same replay of her life in the sessions to follow, I knew that something was wrong, if not with her, then with me. I was bored by the sessions, an unusual thing for me. There were times when I literally had to pinch myself to keep awake. I did not like working with this person very much, despite her efforts to seemingly want to please me as a patient. This forty-three-year-old woman always arrived on time, greeted me cheerfully, dressed neatly, and seemed wholesome and athletic in the way that Girl Scouts are trained to be. Her short-cropped hair and naturally pink, rounded cheeks along with her compact, muscular stature resembled that of a cherub.

My sense was, however, that there was nothing to grab onto, nothing to work with, no feeling or emotion. It was as though her inner life was kept under a sheet of ice upon which I kept sliding. Each time I tried to crack the exterior I fell. And when I collapsed, she threw a thick blanket over me, rendering me useless. I found myself dreading the sessions. Finally I succumbed to the inertia. I accepted the fact that the space she was creating between us had a purpose. I surrendered to it and to her suffocation of me in my effort to understand why she needed to do this to me.

And then it happened. Suddenly one day, after months of her coming to sessions, after multiple attempts on my part to impart some form of empathy or struggle to make an interpretation that seemed appropriate, we clicked.

It happened because I finally went with her into the space she had created for us in that consulting room. I was calm and silent and watchful and open to her experience. I wasn't worrying about knowing anything other than what she was unconsciously trying to tell me. And what was it that she was conveying to me?

It was that she always thought of killing herself. The possibility of suicide had never occurred to me as she repeatedly told me how good her life was and how ungrateful she was for wanting more from it. I was not merely stunned, I was shocked. Obviously my experience of the sessions had not been the same as hers. While I was confused and frustrated and bored by the repetition, she had been taking my measure. Could she confide in me? Could she tell me where she really "lived"?

Her guard at last was down and we were in it. "It" came to be named by both of us as her suicide space. There, she was king of the world, in a place where she could perform any task, no matter how Herculean. She could do anything, be any way that was required of her, because it made no difference how she behaved. In the end, she was going to kill herself anyway. These thoughts of suicide, we came to learn, were necessary for her sterling performances as a wife, mother, daughter and employee of a large company where she held an important leadership position. They were the fuel that fed the adrenalin that fired her actions. Without these thoughts, she could not function to the same degree, therefore she was not willing to let them go.

At this point, being in her inner world was like being a guest in her home. We were home in the one place that mattered to her most. I could only admire what she herself was so proud of: her ability to accomplish tasks and to give advice and direction to her family; her travel to countries around the world as part of her job to teach them company data; her cleverness at solving problems at work and giving away this information to other employees who were given the credit for it; her skill at saving her employer millions of dollars each year by devising foolproof budgets for them; and yes, tragically, her creativity in inventing different methods of killing herself.

Another part of being in her "home" was my feeling of wanting to leave it. I was trapped. It was not as though she had thrown away the key after I entered her space. On the contrary, she did everything she could to push me out. It was more that I could not, would not, remove myself from her because I could not let her die. Whether or not this was a moral issue I do not know. But I do know that I had to fight an all-consuming battle, it turned out, for her life. I was a witness to the insanity. She herself had been a product of evil and insanity.

Her mother had abused her physically and verbally no matter how hard my patient tried to please her. Claire always had a perfect report card and, in fact, won national prizes for projects in science and math. She was star of the girls' basketball team, but when she played against her sister's team, her mother always cheered loudly for Claire's sister instead of Claire. In another attempt to win her mother's love, Claire volunteered to clean the family home which she had done every Saturday since she turned thirteen. This did not help her either. Nothing worked to stop the frequent and unpredictable rages that were only directed at Claire. At these times, Claire would run for the door to escape and continue running through the streets to the subway cars where she would hide, riding the cars all night, alone, frightened, and infused with adrenalin. These episodes became the precursor to her addiction to suicide and to the adrenalin rush, her drug.

I could not walk away once I knew what was there. Was this a rational decision? No. But for me there could be no other one. Claire's attempts at suicide and her addiction to suicidal thoughts went on for years.

I have not liked to impose my work on my husband, but I found that I was doing so in this instance because my work with Claire necessitated that we have contact beyond business hours. Many times her frequent phone calls and my anxiety that she would kill herself took its toll on my personal life.

My husband, my family, my friends were annoyed with me. Whenever I had to leave the room to take a phone call from her, because she was about to jump from a balcony or crash her car into the guard rails of some highway, I was told by family and friends that this was not my job. But because of confidentiality issues, all that I could share was that I had a suicidal patient.

They advised me to turn her over to the authorities. I could not tell them that this had already been done and that she had outsmarted the suicide squad at every turn. My peers, with whom I discussed her case anonymously, told me to call her bluff. They threw theory at me. They looked at me as though they were thinking that I was making mountains out of mole hills or else that I was crazy. It often felt as if it was she and I against a world that could not understand what was going on; nor, more important, did they want to.

Many people have used the expression, "If you can't stand the heat, stay out of the kitchen," but somehow knowing that the psychoanalyst Heinz Kohut quoted it when explaining his theory of self psychology, made perfect sense to me. I had used his technique, empathy, or "being in the shoes of another," when I surrendered any other theory or thoughts I might have had about her. At this point in treatment, I succumbed to letting her do whatever she needed to do in our sessions. If it meant that her resistance to being there would put me to sleep, then I had to weather it. If it meant that she needed to reach me before jumping off a balcony, then it had to be done.

In the first year of treatment, she was taking my measure, while bluffing her way through until she knew what kind of therapist I was. Early on, she had told me that she had been to other therapists before but never stayed because she felt they were not to be trusted. When she was ready to let me into her world because she felt that I could be trusted, she took a giant leap of faith. Then and only then did she allow me to know how things really were in her inner world.

Claire had been placed in a group home when she was sixteen years old at her own request and that of a psychiatrist who briefly saw her parents along with her. While she lived in that home in New York City finishing out her high school years, she met her future husband who had lived there since he was ten years old. They became friends while she continued to excel in school, as well as being a model adolescent in the home. After graduation she was given a scholarship to college, worked hard and was offered a good job in a large company. She again excelled and rapidly advanced in her job. By the time she was twenty-three, they were married and were able to buy a house in the suburbs where their two children were born. Quickly she ascended the corporate ladder and during our work together continued to do so.

Claire's secret was that she constantly thought of killing herself, not out of overt depression as with so many suicidal victims, but because she had got in the habit of using her adrenalin to push herself to the limit. This kind of manic behavior fueled by the rush she got from adrenalin had its rewards for her, but the sense of accomplishment that she achieved did not last long. Her feelings of worthlessness would return and the cycle would repeat itself. On several occasions, she did go over the edge into attempts at killing herself.

At that point, the kitchen became hotter. Did I feel like quitting on her those many times when the kitchen felt as if it were on fire? Not once. All that mattered was that I could not let her die.

Claire did not die. On the contrary, after eighteen years of being in therapy, she is enjoying life to the fullest. What began as a request to have "more fun in her life" has ended in exactly that, but it is life-enhancing fun, not the delight she took in defying death. For many years she was caught in the grip of her addiction, but once she was able to get control over it, her own analysis began.

I cannot, here, go into the many ways we worked together to make this result happen. I have written about our work together elsewhere, and it has been published in other sources. But when her addictive behavior finally stopped, Claire entered her own analysis. All I had to do, in this last stage of treatment, was to sit in my chair and listen to her understand herself. The genetic work, as Heinz Kohut put it, comes last, once empathy has taken its course, and the patient will do it on her own with no need for any but the scantest input from the analyst. Who better to know than the patient herself where she has come from, what has happened to her, how she has tried to live with it and how her attempts at adaptation failed?

* * *

I am not saying that other therapists who might have quit on her would be acting immorally. But I am saying that the marriage between therapist and patient is the most important therapeutic tool that we have. This marriage is complicated and highly individual, as unique as any secular marriage. Negotiations, whether conscious or unconscious, are going on all the time. As with the mother-child unit, the success of the therapeutic partnership depends on how appropriately these accommodations are being managed.

As in most situations, it is important to pay attention to intuition. We may feel that something is not right before we know exactly what that is. We balk. Or we quietly hesitate to move on. But attention must be paid. Often patients idealize the analyst and think that they themselves must be wrong. They need help; therefore, they must be the one who is mistaken. But whoever might be at fault, if the discomfort cannot be spoken of and if attempts cannot be made to understand it, head for the door. Find the right partner for you in this psychoanalytic world. They are out there. It is, in the end, very much like looking for the right spouse.

As for the analysts, so much depends on the quality of their own analysis. How well they understand themselves, their strengths and limitations, are of utmost importance. There is one thing that transcends professional limits and boundaries, and it is called "doing the right thing" by another human being. If that means that the risky patient, the "difficult" one, must be referred elsewhere, so be it. But if there is enough of a union, a connection with that person who has entered your life, then the work becomes heroic and the rewards immeasurable.

CHAPTER TWELVE:

THE DEVIL IS IN THE DETAILS

I've been thinking about when I was trying to be your friend
I thought it was then,
but it wasn't, it wasn't genuine.
~ *Fiona Apple*

We're accustomed to thinking about sexual abuse as being a major cause for concern, a terrible thing that happens to some people. According to a statistic from the Center for Family Justice, 1 out of 4 women and 1 out of 6 men are sexually abused in their lifetime. We hear about individual cases of rape and other forms of violent, non-consensual sexual behavior, and while most of us hope that justice will be served, we generally don't give the matter much thought and go on with our day. Unless, of course, it has happened to us.

Even if it has happened to us, we try not to give it much thought. Sexual abuse is, however, insidious. How like the Medusa's head it is with its many writhing snakes coiling and twisting, penetrating deep inside of us, never knowing whether those snakes will be poisonous and fatal or simply threaten to be so. We'd like not to have to stare at this massive, ugly head, and so we turn away leaving the effects of the abuse to fester within us.

After incidents of sexual abuse, anger is a recurring feeling, as are guilt and shame. We are told that perpetrators must be exposed, but the consequences of exposure can cause us to be ambivalent about "making a fuss." Families in which there is some form of incestuous behavior can be ripped apart. Or, the victim, himself, disbelieved and cast out. And those are only two of the many dire consequences that can occur.

My experience of being sexually abused still remains somewhat of a mystery to me. It has never quite been resolved. Part of this is because even my second analyst failed me when I finally told him my personal history regarding sexual abuse. He, too, misunderstood the power of something that seemed to him not much of anything. I remember him saying, "So he made a play for you." I was not brave enough to confront my analyst, to tell him that he was hurting my feelings by minimizing something that had haunted me for a lifetime. It was time for me to leave him anyway and a few months later, I did.

There is something in therapy that is called "enactment" by certain theorists. It involves both the patient's and the analyst's unconscious and it leads to a stalemate. Recognizing the impasse can be a very useful tool in treatment. Not being able to confront it as I was unable to do, was because I, too, questioned the importance of something that seemed not such a terrible thing. I wasn't raped or tortured, but I had put my trust in someone who betrayed it, who wanted only to dominate and control me. All that I can remember was one kiss, a kiss that startled and frightened me and has stayed with me for a lifetime. But this kiss was not a sign of love or affection. It was more of a bite than a kiss. It was passionate, harsh, and painful. And I was too weak and vulnerable to be able to understand what was happening. The venom it left behind was as potent as if it had almost literally come from the head of the Medusa.

That event stayed with me for most of my adult life as a layer of my skin protecting me from being totally connected with another. It was as if I could go so far and no further, rarely experiencing the freedom of total surrender.

Until I entered analysis when I was 35 years old, I didn't pay a lot of attention to my sexual functioning, as I enjoyed what I knew of making love. Instead, I was met by other problems. Frequently adrift in love relationships,

I allowed myself to be treated badly or taken for granted or betrayed. The betrayal caused me the most pain, and left me rebounding from one inappropriate relationship to another. I'd always thought that it was the men in my life who were incapable of feeling committed to me, but as my analysis continued, I came to believe that the problem was that I was that person, choosing men who could not commit. By doing so, I was unconsciously protecting myself from being seduced yet again by someone professing to care for me while only wanting something for himself.

On the other hand, I was always frightened by anyone who flattered me or admired me. Because I didn't know how to respond, how to feel that I had control in such a situation, I often ran away, feeling fear that verged on panic. The exception was Jean Claude, the French artist, who gently refused to allow me to leave, who at first seduced me with what I thought to be love, although he later abused me with his other loves, alcohol and women.

Over the years, I've come to understand how many varied forms sexual abuse can take. It can range from one single adult kiss on the lips of a child, to an adult emotionally seducing a child, to overhearing throughout one's childhood the sounds of love-making behind thin bedroom walls, to having one child's body be exploited by another; from date rape, to rape at gunpoint; from gang rape, to being fearful of impending rape.

It is expected that actions like rape, or adults seducing children, or individuals becoming enslaved in sex trafficking, will cause suffering. But we don't give much thought to adults emotionally stimulating children if physicality is not present, or of adults who don't maintain the appropriate sexual boundaries. These may seem like minor offenses compared to rape at gunpoint, but their effects may go as deep as far more obvious and violent infringements on another's body.

To examine these "little rapes," as I call them, behavior that pierces through one's psyche as powerfully as the "big rapes," whose destructive power is easier to fathom, I will describe the cases of two of my patients who have been deeply affected by what seemed like "not much." They've further validated my own experience of sexual abuse. One of them, whom I shall call Sara, finds herself always in the role of friend rather than in her wished-for role of girlfriend. She also protects herself by being overweight in order to play the role of wallflower rather than a participant in the dance. Another patient whom I shall call Lisa, had gone from one "bad" man to another.

I believe that any kind of sexual abuse has metabolic powers. The actual events themselves are often so deeply hidden within our psyches and within our bodies that we don't connect our behaviors in the external world (the "details") with the events that caused this behavior. Furthermore, as I've explained, while the details of the event itself often appear to be benign, aspects of our behavior after the event are not. And that is the point.

* * *

A word about confidentiality, my own and that of my patients, is necessary at this point. Secrecy, both at a conscious and at an unconscious level, is an integral component of sexual abuse. It acts to temporarily protect one's self from the offence, and it also serves the purpose of protecting those around us. Secrecy is also the catalyst for conflict. The need to tell versus the need to protect creates a burdensome struggle that cannot easily be resolved. In the following accounts, I have conscientiously tried to balance the two so that we may continue to learn from our experiences, while maintaining the hard-won trust gained in the therapeutic relationship.

It is also important to note that my patients tend to be middle class ranging to upper middle class, and yet their experiences have been those of others who have not been so fortunate economically or educationally. It is not only the isolated, the mentally ill, the uneducated, the rage-infused who inflict themselves on others. Those who abuse can be those who have been abused. Victims tend to create more victims. Silence feeds this form of regeneration. Therapy is a space where this kind of silence can be challenged so that malignancy can be arrested.

* * *

Sara was a big girl, very tall for fifteen years old and slightly overweight when I first met her in 2015. Her gait, as she walked the few feet from the waiting room to my office was slow and lumbering, as if this body of hers was too much to carry. As I watched her move, dragging her feet and keeping her head down, I remember thinking, "Here's another willing/unwilling participant in the process of change." At the same time, I became self-consciously aware of my own barely 5'2" stature which was suddenly making me feel uncomfortable.

We sat and eyed each other in that first session, taking the measure of one another. I sensed her discomfort as I sensed my own. She did not volunteer speaking and when she did, it was in a low voice, difficult for me to hear. As I kept having to ask her to repeat herself, I became even more uncomfortable worrying that she would think this therapist, the therapist that she had fought so hard to get, was deaf.

The result of this almost tangible discomfort in the room was that I knew I must do something quickly to at least put myself at ease, if not Sara. Someone had to be in charge. I knew that Sara had to develop trust with me, and my holding on to the fact that I had seen her mother the week before wasn't the way to do it. Because the session I'd had with her mother was beginning to feel like a guilty secret, I told Sara, rather quickly, what I had done. I explained that her mother was worried because Sara wanted to stay in bed all day and didn't want to go to school or anywhere else for that matter. Sara seemed to simply grunt at this information.

At that time, Sara's mother, an intelligent statuesque woman from the Dominican Republic, was divorced and a single parent of two children. Sara had a brother seven years older who was diagnosed with schizophrenia at about the time of Sara's birth. His behavior often created stress in the family which added to the stress of their mother holding a high powered, highly paid job that came with long hours and a lot of pressure. She was the sole support of her family and of her mother back in the Dominican Republic; neither financially nor emotionally could she afford to make the effort to understand herself or even another child. Besides, hadn't she just been through all of this therapy stuff with her son, who'd been repeatedly hospitalized and wasn't much better after treatment than he'd been before? If she was badly needed, she said, she would come for a session, but only then.

I could sense that this demand was nonnegotiable. I also felt that it was understandable. As a therapist I knew that you couldn't ask a soldier in the middle of a battle to understand what he is feeling for fear that the battle won't get fought. To myself I thought, "It's just you and me, Sara," feeling as though I'd just been given a gift-wrapped package whose contents came with a warning label. Sara and I would work together alone, albeit with her mother's distant support.

Although that first session with Sara did not seem terribly promising, we were at least able to agree on the fact that Sara would rather be at home in her bed under the blankets than be driven to my office for weekly therapy sessions. Because we were able to acknowledge her feelings, Sara agreed that she'd do her best to come. And in fact, in all of our six years together, Sara did not miss one session, behavior that speaks well for her motivation to change.

It also speaks well for a technique called "empathic attunement." Sara's silence was pregnant with meaning. We just did not know of what.

Here is how it worked with Sara. She'd arrive at my office looking obviously anxious. She could not speak. Through this outward appearance of anxiety, I worked to gain entry into her inner world. "Sara," I'd say, "You are anxious today." This comment was greeted by a slight nod. With her seated across from me on the couch, I leaned back in my chair and allowed her silence to enter my mind and to fill it. I tried to imagine what she, in her detachment from me, was feeling. I groped my way around in the darkness, metaphorical arms extended in front of me like a blind man's, until I could see a shadowy door in front of me. Slowly, gently, as though with outstretched index finger, I would push it slightly open until I could understand more of what was happening for her.

If she appeared to be unresponsive to what I thought she was experiencing, I'd move on to try another door. And when I felt that I might be onto something, and tested that feeling by asking her if this was true, I entered the chamber stealthily, on tiptoes, while adjusting to the darkness. A feeling like fear or anger might confront me. These feelings frequently took the form of a bodily feeling such as a constriction in my throat, or my stomach twisting into knots, or a weight on my chest. Then, like a mother teaching her child to speak, I'd put a name to what was being experienced in that moment. Sara could then tell me what the name meant to her, leading us further into her inner world until we arrived at the experience that she had had to repress.

The feeling of being under a heavy weight translated into having the knees of a nine- year-old boy digging into her six-year-old body after he'd wrestled her to the floor. At another time in our exploration of her anxiety, a constriction in my own throat mirrored hers. When I described to her what I was feeling, she told me that during such an encounter he urinated in her face and her open-mouthed screaming only made his form of attack worse.

By putting a name to what I imagined that she, in her detachment from me, was feeling, slowly and step by step we pieced together her experience of having been repeatedly sexually abused by this boy over a one-year period. Sara had been in his home because his mother had been hired to baby-sit Sara after school until her mother returned from work to collect her. The woman probably could not hear the assaults as she was usually downstairs cleaning while listening to a blaring radio. Sara had tried to stop him but, at six or seven, wasn't yet strong enough to fend off the advances of a strong boy three years her senior. She had told her mother about the assaults, and her mother spoke to the boy's mother but the mother did nothing about it. Nothing changed. The two families were related to each other and had always been good friends. The bullying attacks continued until Sara's mother finally was able to make other arrangements for Sara's after-school care.

In my experience it is not unusual for those who are involved in such situations and who are familiar with each other, to miss out on cues and to dismiss ideas that might foretell that something bad is happening. So it was that he, who had been intended for her playmate, turned out to be the executioner of her self-esteem and her pride in herself.

This "play" became the kernel for a pattern of friendship followed by betrayal that had become ingrained for Sara. Time and time again, a person she thought of as a friend turned out to be a monster. This theme was furled and unfurled countless times during treatment. Interestingly what originally brought Sara into treatment was the betrayal of her best girlfriend during her teens. The depression that followed this betrayal would not lift, and that was the event that forced Sara's mother to finally succumb to Sara's repeated requests for help.

After a short time, Sara looked for validation from me that she should end this friendship, one that had turned so cruel because Sara was doing all of the giving and her friend was doing the taking. I gave it, and I marveled at the strength in Sara, the part of her that was emotionally healthy enough to know that being treated badly by a friend was no friendship at all. Then began the flashbacks to the "playmate" who had abused her when she was at a much younger age. And still later, I came to learn of other relationships, especially with her older brother, that frightened Sara with his unexpected explosions of rage and aggression, explosions that left her feeling alone and vulnerable. It was no wonder she felt listless. It was no surprise that she should want to stay in the safety of her own bed. My empathy increased as well as did our mutual anguish at the grisly things that had happened to her.

Our work continued. She and I were together in her horrifying world, but eventually there emerged beautiful Sara, this reluctant, tall, lumbering young woman of many talents who could write exquisite poetry, and design and make cool clothing and drawings. She is now 22 years old and letting me know about her talents, having disowned them in the past. We are currently working with male relationships that are far less problematic for Sara than they have been in the past, while her female friendships have for years now developed into reciprocal ones, supportive and healthy. In fact, these friendships were the first sign that Sara was on her way to recovery. Sara is now in college, doing well, and wanting to be a psychotherapist.

* * *

Good mornin' Good mornin'
You raped me in the same bed your daughter was born in.
~*Fiona Apple*

According to the dictionary, incest is defined as "sexual intercourse between two people who are classed as being too closely related to marry" but the word "incestuous" is defined simply as "sex between people too closely related to marry."

What does sex mean? Does it include what we hear and see as observers of people touching each other? Would we say that Peeping Toms are having a sexual experience by peering through a glass window? Of course we would. So why not understand that when a child overhears the sounds of her parents making love it is akin to forcing a child into being in the same position as a Peeping Tom? And does this have a later effect on that child's behavior that prevents her from freely receiving love and being able to return it? Of course it does. Nonetheless we relegate episodes like this to a misdemeanor rather than a crime.

When my patient, whom I shall call Lisa, phoned to ask for an appointment, she feared that I would not have room for her in my practice. Even after I gave her an appointment for the following week, she was overly effusive in expressing gratitude that I could see her. I registered curiosity about her behavior and was to relive this theme of her not being good enough, of her not being perfect, of her deserving to be an outsider for the next five years she remained in treatment.

"Why can't I get on with this?" Lisa moaned as she told me why she felt she needed help. A pretty 35-year-old who was also a practicing psychotherapist, Lisa was nicely dressed, well-coiffed, and very slightly prim-looking. "I'm stuck," she said. "I have this lovely man who is in love with me and who wants to marry me, and all I can think about when I am with him is how boring he is and how I cannot wait to get home to be alone. He is intelligent, sensitive, generous, and even good-looking. Why can't I enjoy his obvious kindnesses to me? Why do I come home at night and stare into the empty refrigerator and forget why I'm there and close it and wander into the other room and while watching the news on TV see what time it is and realize that I haven't eaten yet? Why is my whole life a question mark? Is this normal at my age?"

These questions were thrown at me like pellets from a BB gun, except that this markswoman paused between shots to loudly blow her nose into the tissues she was tearing out from the box beside her. I lowered my head and murmured, "You feel numb when you're not feeling miserable."

There was a silence. Then Lisa said, "I don't feel anything except when I'm with my patients and feeling for them, or when I'm miserable because I've failed in another relationship of my own. I even failed in the relationship with my past therapist. I've had years of therapy where I talked about my father endlessly. I thought that I'd finished with all of that and still I'm having the same problem of only liking to be with men who mistreat me. I want to have a child, at least I think I do. I don't even know that, but by the time I find out, I'll be past the point of child-bearing."

Lisa then told me that she'd said good-bye to Nicolas, the nice boyfriend, but was now regretting that she had done so. She'd found a new boyfriend about whom she was optimistic until they started fighting over his looking at other women. "This always happens to me," she said, "and it always hurts me and distracts me and saps my energy." I waited for her to go on.

"I think I am so deep down angry," she continued. "I feel that my insides are dark and murky, a sewer. They have this network of subterranean pipes through which excremental mud flows. It has a rhythm of its own. I can't predict it. I can't control it. Can you help me?"

"I want to help you," I replied, aware that I was countering the question. I felt a liking for this young woman who seemed childlike in her need to attach to someone who could accept her messes. I felt encouraged by the fact that Lisa could admit feeling angry even if she couldn't put it into action. On the other hand, I found myself shying away from Lisa's need to idealize me. I'd sensed her need to look up to me in that first phone call, and it was borne out in this first session. Our work had begun.

Lisa's was a story of having a mother who needed Lisa to be her confidante particularly about the sexual relationship she was having with Lisa's father. Because she felt insecure about her looks and her ability to attract her very handsome husband, she defended against those feelings by boasting of her attributes and her husband's love of them when Lisa reached puberty. She needed to let Lisa know how ardent was their love and delighted in sharing the details. What Lisa wasn't told, she could plainly hear through the thin bedroom walls that had since her childhood separated Lisa's room from theirs. As a child she was disturbed by the sounds and tried to stifle them. As she grew older and more beautiful, it was as though her mother had herself torn down the walls by making Lisa her confidante. She talked to her openly about what transpired in the bedroom between her and Lisa's father.

Lisa's father was withdrawn and anxious about his own ability to satisfy his family's needs financially. He owned a string of businesses that were always unpredictable. When they were not doing well, his wife's inheritance would pay the household bills and when they were, the family enjoyed a fine lifestyle. He clung to his wife who bound him to her by telling him how to manage his business and advising him on every aspect of his life. There was no comfortable space for Lisa to be in this household, but Lisa found herself unable to leave home after she'd finished college. As bids to get her father's attention always ended in failure, she accepted her mother's attention even if that attention was all about her mother.

This mother needed her daughter to be perfect in every way. Most of all, she needed her to be a "good girl," which meant listening to her mother talk about herself, obeying her in her choice of clothing and college and "not bothering" her father, thereby increasing the distance between them. Lisa was caught between alternately complying and rebelling against this uneasy threesome and her mother's need for her. And perhaps unsurprisingly, when her anger erupted, she threw herself into the arms of men who were emotionally unavailable to her.

I frequently left the office thinking about Lisa. Her pattern with men had been so similar to my own that I had to work overtime on myself to separate out what belonged to me and what was hers. In sessions with her I felt such anguish that I had to restrain myself from advising her or admonishing her for repeating the destructive behavior. She had one inappropriate relationship after another. They had all started out like fireworks, bright and overwhelming, filling the entire space that she occupied. With each one she was convinced that she had found a man who loved her until his attention was drawn to other women, or, sometimes worse, relentlessly drawn to her flaws and faults.

My job was to bear witness. She had more than enough advice that only served to make her feel worse about herself. Besides, it was easy for Lisa to understand what she was doing intellectually while avoiding feeling, something that throughout her life she had been taught to do. So I listened and felt with her. Sometimes I interpreted, but mostly I just waited.

In a moment of emotional clarity, Lisa broke off with that "bad" fellow who had replaced the good Nicolas. She was able to say that he was the imperfect one, a real "loser who couldn't even support himself." She then told me, "I've always felt that something set me apart from people, some dirty secret. So I kept my distance from people whom I felt to be 'healthy,' 'nice,' 'normal.' It was as if I was afraid of contaminating them, so I didn't let them get too close to me."

Shortly after that, Lisa resumed the relationship with Nicolas who had patiently waited for her return. She was beginning to see him in a new light when a great job offer came her way. The job required that she move across the country. She took it. She and Nicolas had to part. She and I had to part.

I may never know the end of Lisa's journey. I wish I could say that between us we slayed the head of the Medusa and watched it roll away. I am left wondering if we had been successful. I had given her the tools: the shield, the mirror, the sword. Nonetheless, she had to find her own way. I am grateful, however, to have known such a persevering human being who, I believe in my gut, will not give up until she finds her own peace.

* * *

In both these cases, only the patient knew that something was not right with them. They couldn't define it, but they wanted to exorcise it. Others were telling them to ignore what they were feeling and move on, or were telling them that nothing had happened, or, if it had, "not much" had happened. These two women tried hard to believe what they were told by well-intentioned people because it is not only uncomfortable to be the voice of dissension, but it is also difficult to know if the situations really happened, so bizarrely clandestine as they had been. Being victimized can also be experienced as alienating, can be lonely making, even feel "crazy making."

Had they accepted the opinion of others, they would have looked square in the face of Medusa and been turned to stone. But by being given back their own reflection, they became empowered by their experience.

Psychoanalysis can be the home of the Gorgons, a place where monsters roam. But it can also be with the help of a Perseus, the therapist, the guide, the witness, whatever we want to call her–the place where our own truth is reflected back to us, making us the individual that we are.

Therapy is about learning one's own truth, owning it and finding ways to deal with it. We should be able to say at the end of it: This is who I am. This is what happened to me. And finally, this is me, free of whatever interfered with me. I can now walk without limping. I can even add a skip to my step.

CHAPTER THIRTEEN:

ABOUT EVIL

Decades ago, as a young adult living with the French painter, Jean Claude, on the Greek island of Symi in the house overlooking the Aegean Sea, I heard one of our French guests use an expression that sounded like, "Souffrir et mourir sans parler." Roughly translated it means "to suffer and to die without speaking."

I was in my twenties and I did not bother to unravel the meaning of the phrase. I had returned to Symi after a brief stint working as a school social worker in upstate New York. My divorce was in the past, and, with my newly earned money, I had rented a large elegant mansion boasting many balconies and long French doors and windows facing the port. It had been the home of an exporter of natural sponges, something the island was known for until the invention of synthetic sponges put the entire island, divers and merchants alike, out of business. My intention was to settle there with Jean Claude indefinitely. I was trying to learn to speak French the way the French spoke the language. I was trying to follow complicated conversations about art and relationships–mistresses and lovers and family backgrounds–and also swimming in the majestic turquoise sea. I was not thinking. I was taking in this island, the people who lived there, and those who visited us with all of my senses. I was smiling always, while trying to keep my feet planted firmly on the cool marble floors beneath them.

Overtime, that phrase spoken in French kept returning to me like the sound of a ship's bell in a fog. But I was able to decipher its meaning only recently, when I connected the quote to the concept of evil. To suffer and to not speak of the pain that has caused that suffering enables evil to go on existing unopposed. I have learned this from my patients, both those who inflict pain on themselves and those who inflict pain on others. And I have learned this from my own personal experience.

That word "evil" is not only difficult to say. It is also difficult for anyone to hear, let alone witness. "Devil" is another word that evokes strong reactions. Perhaps it is meant to give evil an image, a face, so that we may better understand it, but that image does not work for me. In fact, no image does that except those offered me by my patients as they tell their stories of the cruelty and abuse inflicted on them or as they shout out their hatred and describe their cruelty towards others. I am not a theologian, nor, quite honestly, did I ever give much thought to the concept of evil until the later years of my practice, when I have come to know when I am in the presence of evil. Yet tragically, it is there that psychoanalytic theory has no effect. Nor is my love for the patient enough, and all of my feelings of uselessness as a therapist are in full force.

Psychoanalysts are particular witnesses to evil. Evil resides in sexual abuse as well as in any other form of abuse. It resides in hatred. It thrives through lies. It loiters in addictive behavior, waiting to overtake the addict when addiction becomes extreme. Lying, or denying, or projecting our feelings of self-hatred toward others, or even avoiding our feelings, are hand -maidens of evil. When we cannot extricate ourselves from these behaviors, evil is allowed in. And once evil is able to grab onto us, it will not easily let go.

Dr. M. Scott Peck, a psychiatrist, psychoanalyst and author of the 1983 bestseller, *People of the Lie: The Hope for Healing Human Evil,* writes about evil as being "in opposition to life." He continues: "It is that which opposes the life force. It has to do with killing...killing that is not required for biological survival." He goes on to say, "Evil is also that which kills spirit . . . essential attributes . . . such as...growth, autonomy and will." (M. Scott Peck, M.D., People of the Lie, 1983). These statements capture the emotions I have witnessed in my consulting room better than anything else I have ever read. Such experiences of "killing" are what give evil its wings, and its landing place is in our inner world. There, it has no voice until we therapists and patients prod it into painful existence. Then, the toxic mix of experiences like cruelty, neglect, manipulation and abuse that have had to be repressed may eventually find their release.

It is ironic, however, that patients who come to our consulting rooms with all good intentions of trying to understand why they are uncomfortable in their lives are often unable to speak. We are confronted by silence. And so begins the work of learning to read the symptoms of their unhealthy behavior that eventually may lead to a path to their inner world, their unconscious world. By recognizing and unraveling self-destructive or "strange" actions, a chink appears through which the repressed material can begin to surface.

There is another kind of silence kept in place by patients who speak openly of their hatred towards others and the cruelty they would like to inflict, or are in fact inflicting. For those who cannot admit to any damage done to themselves, silence is maintained by attempting to "kill" others whether physically, emotionally, or spiritually.

Carl Jung, the Swiss psychiatrist and psychoanalyst who founded the concept of analytical psychology, was one of the great explorers of the human psyche. Although I am not a particular follower of his, he has helped me understand our inability to stem the pain we inflict upon one another and upon ourselves. "The Shadow personifies everything that the subject refuses to acknowledge about himself," he writes, "and yet is always thrusting itself upon him directly or indirectly" (Jung, 1968, Coll. Works, Vol. 9, p.284). The Shadow is the dark, unknown, side of our personality, hidden away from conscious knowledge because it can be unappealing, even ugly.

The Shadow is a part of our unconscious mind. And, like Death, it is out there behind us, stalking us unseen. An inevitable part of our existence, it is as elusive as a poltergeist. When we try to catch and hold our Shadow, it repeatedly slips out of our grasp. Grab it and it dissolves. The only real weapon we have is to try to embrace our Shadow and drag its contents out into consciousness. As Jung puts it, "To confront a person with his own shadow is to show him his own light" (Jung, Good and Evil in Analytical Psychology, 1959). To confront the hidden parts of ourselves, those parts that we do not like about ourselves, and even those parts that we would like if we were able to embrace them as our own natural needs, is not only to salute our own truths but also to attempt fighting evil.

The concept of the Shadow becomes even more complicated when Jung goes on to say that the Shadow consists not only of repulsive and shameful tendencies but also instincts which naturally protect us. "It can be ascertained that the unconscious man, that is, his Shadow, does not consist only of morally reprehensible tendencies," he writes," but also displays a number of good qualities, such as normal instincts, appropriate reactions" (Jung, Coll. Works, Vol. 9, p. 266). Those emotions can be fear, anger, desire, need. These can serve to protect us while encouraging growth, but they may also prevent us from acting in ways that help others. Behavior that might be useful for protecting ourselves, might cause damage to others especially those who are in great need of protection. Tragedy is made up of messages from the Shadow that we are unable to decipher. We act instinctively, without thinking, and this behavior can result in good or bad.

We try. We therapists who have been analyzed and therapized, we try to acknowledge our fears and prejudices, our counter-transferences. But we cannot analyze what we do not know to be there. Until we are confronted by a situation that arouses our unconscious Shadow, we cannot bring it into consciousness. Instinctively, we can be in the grip of something that we need to deny. We feel something that we do not allow ourselves to feel. Yet these reactions are appropriate because they are protective of ourselves, at least in the short term.

We have all heard of social workers who have been fired and disbarred from their profession because a child has been molested or starved or beaten to death under their supervision. We rush to judge them for their incompetence. What they are instinctively doing, however, is protecting themselves from the evil that they are sensing in a household in which a child has been abused. Rather than stay and fight what they see, they are unconsciously ignoring the signs of horror, as subliminal as they may be.

How does it happen that there is one mass shooting after another despite our efforts to understand and stop such horrors? What happens when one day we have a patient in our office talking rationally about the suicide of his son and the next day, we receive a phone call from his family that he, the father, has shot himself in the head? Clearly signs of catastrophe are not being picked up. Is it because suicide fills us with such horror that we must look away from it and in so doing, give it permission to exist? As with cruelty, hatred, and intense mental torture?

It is generally known that where there has been one suicide in a family, there is a likely to be another. And when there have been two suicides in a family, there may be a third. Many people know of this phenomenon, but it is really hard to think about, in the same way that it is hard to think about mass murder, the Holocaust, and the killing that is part of war.

Such things happen, we tell ourselves. Everybody reads about these tragedies online or in the newspapers. Television newscasts are taken up with them for a day or two, but they are quickly forgotten. We gasp and move on and away from them because we are unable to confront the evil inherent in these events. "It is quite within the bounds of possibility for a man to recognize the relative evil of his nature," Jung writes," but it is a rare and shattering experience for him to gaze into the face of absolute evil"(Collected Works, 9ii, para. 14)

Evil seems to go beyond psychological theory. In fact, my experience has been that in extreme cases of repression caused by extreme abuse, theory is of little use. Out of a sense of respect for patients who have come to me with intense fears about behavior that they cannot control, I force myself to write about such behavior. How well we uproot these experiences of extreme repression, experiences that remain not only in our inner world but also in our bodies, will determine whether evil is being challenged instead of fostered. We must suspend any sense of disbelief we might have regarding evil and go to the place where the patient lies in torment. There we might find the answers as to how to ease and ideally dispel this torment.

I extend my deepest apologies to the patients from whom I learned of the existence of evil and whom I failed in this regard. In the presence of evil, I have been so confused that I could not name what I was experiencing and as a result evil was allowed to go on existing. I have been filled with shame and regret over the few instances in my career when I encountered evil, but could not fight against something I could not name at that time. Out of desperation, people came to me for help, and I, in my ignorance, could not give it to them.

In one such case, a mother withdrew her son from treatment under a false pretext, the real reason, I expect, being that I could not empathize with her hatred of her child. At some level I am certain that she understood that. In the other case, yet another suicide occurred in a family that had already had too many. In that situation, evil was being kept alive by the hostility between the parents of the children who killed themselves. Unexamined anger is a potent ingredient for killing both body and spirit.

* * *

I too have a shadow, in various shades of gray. Despite the fact that I have had a total of two analyses for a total of 17 years along with 46 years of clinical experience. I feel that I could have done more for a child who was brought to me for help by his mother. The use of empathy as a technique brought me to the brink of understanding evil, but evil outsmarted me and whisked the child out of treatment just as he was showing signs of progress. That pattern is not unusual. Working with children is a complicated dance involving work with both the parents and the child, and establishing a rhythm, a beat, where all three can dance together. Balance is of utmost importance. If one part lags behind another, all the partners can be pulled down. But in the case I am about to describe, evil prevailed in spite of all of the parts working together. The mother waltzed off the dance floor, and the treatment ended.

* * *

Mothers are supposed to love their children; but one mother who came to my office taught me that this does not always happen. She told me that her 10-year-old son, Todd, enraged her. She had two other children, whom she described as "wonderful," as "golden" children whom she could be proud of. But Todd was an embarrassment to her. She could not understand why his teacher had no problems with him. Todd's mother had visited the school on numerous occasions to tell his teachers how bad he was, only to be told that he was doing fine in the classroom both socially and academically. She was certain that the teachers were wrong and spoke of sending the child to private school.

All of this information was relayed to me in that first session, when I see the parent or parents without the child being present, and in the second session, when I see the child alone. At the time, I was winding down in my career, and although I felt as if I were being presented with an intractable "bad seed," I also felt competent as an analyst and up for the challenge.

The mother said that Todd had been behaving badly ever since the day he was born, but only now, at 10, when he could find ways to embarrass her in public, did she feel the need for help. In addition, Todd's father was beginning to be upset by his son's behavior. I asked to see father, but I was told that his work as an international business consultant required that he be away from home frequently. The mother, however, was agreeable to the idea of being seen in separate, alternating sessions from Todd's.

A pretty woman always dressed in the latest trend, she told me that every family vacation was disrupted by Todd, because he shouted over people, wouldn't thank them or would slobber over his food in public and embarrass her. He insisted on wearing the wrong clothes and as a result never looked fashionable like the rest of the family. Getting him to shower or brush his teeth always involved a fight. He lied. He cheated at games and cards. He was clumsy, falling easily or spilling things. Recently he had begun to touch his private parts in public. This last detail was reported in a voice without emotion, as if this behavior were no worse than his other behaviors. He did get along with his other siblings, but he was beginning to act out with his father.

In individual sessions with me, Todd, a nice-looking, tow-headed ten-year-old, behaved in the way his mother had described. He came with me easily into the treatment room as if he was eager to know what therapy was all about. Once there, however, he sat nervously in the exact center of the couch looking around at everything in the room, wanting to know what was in my desk drawers and in the closet behind me.

Usually I will refrain from directly answering such questions, but in this case I felt that it was too soon to appear to be withholding and so quickly showed him the inside of the closet where my filing cabinet was kept while explaining the need for patient confidentiality and why I could not tell him more. He continued to be insistent about wanting to see more, but I observed that he did so with a kind of tongue-in-cheek attitude.

Finally, he gave in and said that he wanted to play cards with me. He soon began to cheat and combined his performance with touching his private parts while looking directly at me with an expression of quiet defiance as if to say, "Do you see me? What are you going to do about it?" When I commented on his behavior by saying gently, "You look pleased that you are able to do this," I was greeted with silence. I would continue, saying something like, "No one can really prevent you from doing so. That has to be a good feeling, Todd. You must feel free."

At the beginning of our work during these times, he would smile, look straight at me, and continue to do what he was doing. Then, after a few more sessions and more of my commenting on his behavior, he stopped. He didn't want to play cards anymore, he said. He wanted to draw. Previously he had refused every offer I had made to have him draw as I find drawings a useful way of entering into a child's inner world. When he asked to draw, I was caught by surprise and was inwardly delighted. After this, we began to converse together. He liked swimming. So did I. He liked going out to eat. Me too. We were developing a relationship. I learned that he was drawing pictures to take home to his mother, but I noticed that she did not look at them when he excitedly handed them to her at the end of the session.

When Todd began treatment, the initial reports from home were that he was showing slight signs of improvement, but as our relationship deepened, very different reports were offered. With each session during this time of our growing relationship, his mother's rage and desperation increased until, she told me, she could hardly bear to be in the same room with him. He disgusted her, she said. And perhaps understandably, the more that Todd felt his mother's contempt, the more he acted in ways that she despised.

We never reached a point of resolution. After a dozen sessions, Todd was taken out of treatment. I was told that there was some problem with scheduling, but we both knew that was not the real issue. The mother was frightening herself and me with her unchecked rage. When she suggested that Todd be sent to live away from the family with an aunt who was childless, I surrendered to this decision because we both knew that Todd needed to be away from her. He was fighting hard not to be destroyed, but how long could this child maintain his own sanity given this toxic relationship with his mother? How long would it be before he was unable to stop the behavior he was taunting her with?

Todd's mother, for her part, was tortured by her feelings about her son. She had tried to do something about them by coming for help. But the help that she seemed to be asking for was validation that Todd was indeed hateful. The two other children at home were not. She seemed to be saying, "I am a good mother for them. It is Todd's fault that I cannot love him as I do the others."

I could not validate that conclusion for her. Instead I wanted her to understand her feelings by looking at her marriage and her own childhood. But each time that she was led toward doing that, her response was that both were perfect and thus there was no point of entry. Her childhood had been flawless, she told me, as was her marriage—except for these problems with their son. Her husband was beginning to get exasperated, too, she told me.

I felt empathy for Todd, and for his mother's spiraling feelings. I also felt powerless, defeated and ashamed that because of her decision to end therapy, I was not being allowed to continue trying to resolve these problems. Would things have gone differently if I had thought in terms of evil rather than trying to fit all these behaviors into a psychological framework? I think so. I see that now. Psychologically the mother needed to defend herself from seeing that her marriage was imperfect and that she was fearful of it being destroyed. I can only guess at this conclusion as she would not discuss the subject. I do know that the more she could not let go of this defense, the more that Todd was scapegoated and, the more she became a victim of Todd's "badness".

I think that I should have understood that the mother was unable to rid herself of her convictions. That yes, in some way she was so obsessed with thinking that her child was evil that her perception became real for her. She said as much to me. Yet I didn't, couldn't, follow her into her reality. It was too unheard of, too unnatural for a mother to talk of her young child with hate, especially when this child had committed no other crime than that of being undesirable to his mother.

Besides, weren't his behaviors explicable psychologically? He had become her victim. His mother made him so uneasy that he did spill his food and he did speak out of turn and cheat to see how others would respond. It is likely that he had started touching himself as a way of both comforting himself and getting his mother's attention. There are many differing hypotheses. I shall never know which was the correct one. But had I accepted the fact that a mother could indeed hate her child, as this one did, we might have established some truth. We could have worked forward from there.

The reasons for the child being removed from his family were not in essence the true ones. Yes, his behavior was bad, but it was a reaction to the hatred he was sensing from his mother. Unfortunately, by trying to defend himself, he was incriminating himself further.

Still, he was only a child. He couldn't yet figure that out. He was too involved in trying to connect with his mother in some way, in any way, so that she would relate to him. Bad as the connection was, Todd needed it. He needed a mother. What he would have benefitted from, of course, would have been her love. Even I, the analyst, found it hard to like, not him but his mother, especially at first. She was not cooperating with treatment, making it difficult for me to give her what I had been taught would help her. Had I accepted her real plight, her fears and her need to defend against them, I might have liked her, too, and things might have gone differently. I should have accepted the fact that a mother can hate her child, and that in some instances it is beyond the mother's power to act differently. I could have loved her for her struggle in the face of something greater than herself. Maybe then we could have halted the massacre of this poor innocent child.

I will always wonder how Todd developed. I would bet that his mother's noble act, as evidenced by her sending him away from her to keep him safe, combined with his natural ability to fight for survival have put him in a better place than she, his mother, is able to be in. She was caught in the grip of something greater than herself. I feared for her.

* * *

When I first heard that phrase, "to suffer and to die without speaking," I was not talking very much, whether in English, Greek or French. I was inhibited by my ignorance of the "foreignness" around me and so I kept quiet while nonetheless being observant. Therefore, at first I thought the phrase referred to my own silence. I have always been a quiet person, a born observer of whatever it is around me, but as a child I learned not to speak my observations out loud. My mother had taught me the cliched idea that if you had nothing nice to say, say nothing at all. But even when I said nice things, she appeared not to be listening.

Still, there was more than that going on. I have a photo of myself taken when I was about 18 months old. I was seated with my brother on a table in a photographer's studio. My brother has his arm about me protectively as he would metaphorically continue to do throughout our lives. I stare out at the camera with a pensive expression. He has a slight, sweet smile on his face. I have none. Serious and soft-looking at the same time, I was already trying to understand the world. The slightly puzzled look foretold that I would be in search of ways to solve the mysteries I would encounter.

As I grew into childhood, I witnessed or overheard things that I could not understand, as I am sure all children do, but there are some children who can dismiss such things and go on playing with their toys while others absorb them. Those episodes seem to be hidden in a reservoir somewhere deep within the psyche. A good name for that place is the inner world. We all have one. We all have recurring fears and thoughts that we will not talk about. Sometimes this is because we are unable to find words for them, other times because they have been pushed down so far that it takes an acute disturbance in the outer world to shake them into activity again. These disturbances are what psychotherapists call "triggers".

There were many times in my childhood when unspeakable, incomprehensible events occurred. My feeling was invariably one of discomfort that was sometimes mixed with fear. But if my brother was there to help me handle the episode, it would become a conscious memory and did not disappear into that inner world. That was a good thing. I then had an image that I could hold onto and the discomfort would disappear.

I remember, for example, the summer night when my mother left us alone with a babysitter. I was five, my brother, eight. My father had died just a few months before, and this was the first time that my mother left us after his death. The teenager who was our babysitter had boyfriends who came to visit her. She talked to them through the screens on our side porch while my brother and I played together. Then suddenly one of the boys began yelling and tearing at the screen that separated him from us. I didn't understand what he was doing, or why, but he seemed violently angry. Something terrible was happening. I saw the babysitter's terror-stricken face and her helplessness. I moved closer to my brother, who then ran into the kitchen to telephone our uncle for help.

Fortunately my mother was at our uncle's home and swiftly returned to ours. Action was taken. The boys fled. I felt relieved. And so, this episode has remained a vivid memory to me, a part of my reality. It is a story that I have told myself again and again. A story about a smart brother who protected and loved me. I could make sense of what had happened. It became a part of my spoken history and of my love for him.

There were other times, however, when that feeling of discomfort was present but no action was taken to relieve it. I would pick up the sound of something without understanding the sense of it, or see something inexplicable. I would look to my mother for an explanation, but I would get none. She was either too busy with other things or too frightened to deal with my questions. And so she ignored my small hand groping for hers.

The troubling words that I had heard, that I had pricked up my ears to hear, went into that repository that I have spoken of, that pit of the inner world where they would eventually be "forgotten." Or I would see things that I would want to move away from. Things that no one mentioned but were nonetheless going on. For example, my fifteen-year-old stepsister turned pale and began shaking whenever her father entered the room. I still do not know what might have transpired between them, but I do know that his look at her was always severe, too severe for this pale quiet child who seemed too timid to misbehave.

Again, there was that feeling of discomfort, a sense that something had just happened that felt strange. I looked away, wishing that I had not seen it. But I did want to know what was going on. It was as though I covered my eyes with outstretched fingers so that I could see, but not. Then there would be an accompanying litany in my mind—"Did it happen? Did it not?"–until I moved on to not thinking about the episode at all. These episodes remained somewhere in my bones, in my body, in my inner world. Nonetheless, silence had been maintained.

It was not until my first analysis in England and after I had started working as a psychotherapist in London, that my silence was described to me with an image that I could grasp. "You keep your light under a bushel," my analyst said to me one day as if out of nowhere. I absorbed that statement as a compliment with no hidden meaning. I felt embarrassed and at the same time proud that anyone, and especially my learned analyst, could think that I had anything to say.

Eventually I forgot that she had described me in this way. But I began to realize that all of the ideas that had made up my adult life, were not mine but my husband's or Jean Claude's. Chameleon-like, I did not have any opinions of my own to speak of. The same was true when it came to my friends, my colleagues, my family back in America. In this way, I created my own sort of exile, forever on the outside looking in with no one really knowing me, let alone able to relate to me; except in terms of whatever they needed me to be for them. I was an object. If I was anything else, it was invisible to me and, I felt, to them.

So I began speaking up. At first tentatively, voice trembling, barely speaking above a whisper. This didn't get me very far, but it was good practice. And as I continued in this way, I grew stronger, more focused on what I was saying rather than on the "me" who was saying it. I gradually noticed that people were listening to me. I was astounded, so much so that for a while I could not take in their comments because I was still stunned that I had spoken and been heard. So at that time, I finished the French quote by saying, "To suffer and to die without speaking would have been a wasted life." I had a voice. I was euphoric with the power of the spoken word.

Although the psychoanalyst is in a unique position to become acquainted with evil, such behavior rarely goes by that name. I am writing about evil because that word must be spoken. To die without speaking of evil would be irresponsible of me. To find ways of fighting evil we must first accept the fact that it exists and then recognize its presence when we experience it. Calling it what it is, is the first step. Understanding it is wisdom. Fighting it is courageous.

CHAPTER FOURTEEN:

AND SO IT GOES

One day this past winter when I was walking the road that fringes the lake near our house in the northern Adirondacks in upstate New York, where my husband and I now live, I saw etched on a snow-covered boulder, one I pass on my daily walks, the words, "I love Bev." There is rarely a car on that road in winter, as only a handful of people live in this wilderness. Nor is there ever a sound, except for the occasional call of a woodpecker and, sometimes, the hush of the wind. In the silence, I paused where I stood, a smile flickering on my face, and my heart glowing.

We usually do not walk together, he and I. He walks faster than I do, challenging his own speed. I walk more slowly, marveling at the sparkling snow carpeting the road and lying in great marshmallow dollops around the trunks of bare trees or resting heavily on the pine branches. Except for my eyes, which stay watchful when I travel my four miles, I am drawn within. And when I speak out loud, it is to God. That day, I thanked Him for those words written on that whitened rock and went on my way feeling as if I had found a precious love note in a bottle at the bottom of the sea. A buried treasure.

My husband is usually neither demonstrative, nor does he talk about his emotions. Because he does not usually show his love in obvious ways, in my younger years, I would have thought that he did not love me, and would have experienced his behavior as my inadequacy, unattractiveness, and unworthiness. And because of that, we probably would have been at odds with each other, and I would never have been in receipt of that snowy love note.

I can no longer destroy myself by intoning a litany of my shortcomings as I did in the past. My newly gained self-esteem simply cannot entertain them anymore. Well before I was analyzed, when I was in my late teen years, my mother looked at me once, and said irritably, "If only you knew how beautiful you are." The words were spoken with anger and impatience as though I were too dense to understand the meaning of what she was telling me—and I was. I took it as a rebuke, because I could not feel that I was beautiful.

I have changed from being that insecure woman. I'm now able to experience my husband's undemonstrativeness as being characteristic of him, even part of his charm, and as having nothing to do with me. It has left me to feel free in our relationship, free to be myself, so at ease with him that I catch myself wondering in the old way, if my sometimes childish, silly pranks are not off-putting to him. But when I see him trying to keep a straight, serious face that gives way to irresistible laughter, I know that they are not.

Yes, there are still times when I feel unsure of myself. Psychoanalysis cannot take away the experiences that formed such a big part of me, but it can reduce the effect of those experiences by putting them into an understandable context, and unearthing the feelings that had gone dead around them. And for that and so much else, I am grateful.

Gratitude is a word that I have come to understand better since having been analyzed, but I am timid about using that expression, as it has become trivialized in contemporary use. I am even more timorous about using the name, God. Yet the two terms have somehow become connected for me. Perhaps my reluctance in using such charged words is because I am unable to explain how I have come to believe in Him so deeply. All I know is that my belief, and the spirituality that accompanies it, have been an unexpected, unasked for, result of my analysis.

This does not mean that I have become religiously observant, even though my husband follows the traditions of the Jewish faith, and I have learned to follow some of those customs from him. It simply means that I have come to believe in the idea of God—for me, a personal, universal God, to whom I feel irrefutably connected. It is to Him that I am grateful for the gifts given me in this life.

I cannot say that analysis results in a belief in God for everyone. That would be absurd, and besides, I cannot know what other people experience. My faith is a recent phenomenon. It has been with me, growing gradually, sneaking up on me, for just a few years. It did not come in a Hallelujah moment, although Hallelujah is certainly an appropriate response to having received it.

This hallelujah response, whispered under my breath, is a spontaneous one. There have been other occurrences that have appeared in my life spontaneously, naturally, slipping in quietly after all of those years of wanting them to happen. That the changes are a result of having been analyzed, I have no doubt. Although it seems as if some of these transformations have been a long time in coming, they are the result of the internal structural change that is the goal of psychoanalysis.

There is no cause and effect result in psychoanalysis or in psychoanalytic therapy. Unlike medicine, where a pill is given that is known to have a desired result, psychoanalysis works in far less linear ways. The movement towards change is a back-and-forth one. Put another way, psychoanalysis can be compared to climbing a mountain by spiraling upwards around it, arriving at a higher point with each step. The same signpost is being passed, call it the symptom, but it is seen from a slightly different perspective as the climb grows higher, until that signpost is out of sight because the top of the mountain has been reached.

The trajectory for change, therefore, is a difficult one to trace as it is gradual, and it mostly exists at a level below consciousness. And in any case, trying to trace it always seems to end with the old chicken-and-egg problem. Was I one of those people who were born in a state of spiritual "grace," or did "grace" come to me as a result of being in such close proximity with my analysts, the result of the melding between the two of us? Did my spiritual yearning begin as I lay in that field in the woods so many decades ago looking up at the sky for my father? Did it continue when, as a child of eleven, I wrote in my dark blue leather diary with the lock on it that I still keep in my desk drawer, "I want wisdom. I want it to radiate out from me like the rays of the sun."

Or did my spiritual yearning emerge because over time my analysis cleansed me of my anger, which was either directed at myself, or repressed and therefore out of reach, but nonetheless hanging over me like a dark cloud preventing me from experiencing my faith? Perhaps was it because psychoanalysis broke down my defenses, sometimes gently, sometimes not, so that I could look beneath them to discover what it was they were protecting me from?

I was not brought up with any religion, much to my grandmother's disapproval. My mother rebelled against her mother's wish to have us raised in the Jewish faith, even though my grandmother was flexible in her practice of religion. Growing up, surrounded by white Christians in a genteel country town, my mother wanted to blend in with the others, as first generation immigrant's children are likely to do. In fact after sending me to Sunday school for a year when I was in the third grade, my mother decided that fresh air would do me more good than sitting in a classroom and studying religion. I was disappointed. I was reading *Little Women* at the time, and I wanted to continue wearing my one Sunday-best blouse and green corduroy jumper the way those legendary New England sisters did on a Sunday. It was not until I was a teenager that I noticed the stack of books on my mother's bedside table, a mix of works by Norman Vincent Peale, the minister best known for promoting the power of positive thinking, along with tracts from the Jehovah's Witnesses given to her by our next door neighbor, himself a Witness, and the Old Testament. I never asked her about them, although I wanted to.

Then there were the mindless walks to the monasteries on the island of Symi. But it wasn't until after I began my first analysis in England that I found myself again seeking out the odd church or synagogue on a Holy Day. It didn't matter to me if the holiday was a Christian or Jewish one. I would find a place of worship that welcomed me, a lonely and self-conscious stranger, where I could think about and be in contact with God, although the next day I would have forgotten about Him again.

Seeds of my spiritual growth were planted bit by bit, separated from each other by gaps and years, but through the process of psychoanalysis they were brought together to form a coherent whole. Carl Jung writes of psychoanalysis as having a transformative formation, like the one of alchemy, that takes place between patient and analyst. Such pairing results in a product that could not have been foreseen, as it includes the unconscious and the conscious minds of each, that is, both the known and the unknown. I certainly feel that my transformation, now that I am looking so closely at the changes that have taken place in my psyche, is partially the result of this process.

I have spoken earlier of the test tube wherein patient and analyst are enclosed in an extremely intimate relationship in which each affects the other, as happens in intimate relationships. The results of this unique pairing are as mysterious as any kind of birth, or creation, and they affect both participants.

Jung uses the word, "individuation" to define the process of the attainment of Self, of wholeness, of our own individual uniqueness. He describes its formation as being the goal of a successful psychoanalysis. "Individuation means becoming a single, homogeneous being," he wrote, and, "in so far as 'individuality' embraces our innermost, last, and incomparable uniqueness, it also implies becoming one's self . . . coming to selfhood or self-realization."

* * *

Meanwhile without any signs of alchemy in evidence in the room—or of Carl Jung—I came to mourn my dead father during my first analysis. It was painfully hard work, but it resulted in my knowing him as if he had still been alive. In retrospect I believe that that process returned to me a piece of myself that had been missing. It enlarged me, expanded me in the way that "normal" children get to know a father through what are called introjects, that is, by incorporating his ideas and attitudes into their personality without being consciously aware of doing so. In fact, I was brought closer to knowing all the "hims" in my life by better knowing my own experience of having had my father. I finally had something that I could measure other men by. For those who have grown up with a father, this is a part of normal development. For me, coming to know my father was established through psychoanalysis even decades after his death.

When I was a teenager and anyone asked me about my father, I would simply say that he was dead. Such a flat retort usually thumped to the ground like a piece of rotted wood. The embarrassed questioner would automatically say, "Sorry." To which I would flippantly, stupidly, respond, "No, you are not, nor am I. You didn't know him, and neither did I." Such a response now fills me with shame. It was a lie, and one that was surely harmful to me who had spent my childhood searching for my father in the heavens, and utterly rude and offensive to anyone else.

Psychoanalysis has removed all of that defensive cutting off of feelings. The loss of my father when I was four years old was more than I could bear, but no one ever spoke to me about it. No one. It seemed to me that the message given me was a persistent "Help your mother to get through her loss and you can do that by being "good." It was expected that I didn't feel a sense of loss because I was too young to understand death, and because I was a child, I could not put into words what I felt. Even my brother, could not be articulate about his loss. He eventually acted out his despair by behaving "badly," displaying behavior that caught the attention of the adults who then tried to help him. I simply went along with being the "good" child and lived vicariously, albeit unconsciously, through his being "bad." He cried a lot, especially under the shower where he might have thought we couldn't hear him. I think it was the showers' warmth and the steam enveloping him that felt like a needed, comforting embrace that permitted him to give vent to his grief.

Now, after all of these many decades, I have my father back within me. All that I had introjected from him, all that I had unconsciously internalized, remains intact, crystalline, in my psyche. And there is more about him that I have pieced together since. I had always been told by my mother that my father would lie on the couch on Saturday afternoons and listen to opera on the radio. Or, he would be playing the piano, or a game of golf, or fishing somewhere locally. Never did he play at vigorous sports or was he part of a sports team, although his physique was certainly muscular and athletic-looking. Posthumously, I have thought that he did so to hide his handicap from others, and from us, giving him more of a sense of control over something that he had not. I also can imagine that he was quietly shoring up a supply of funds, which he succeeded at doing, that would take us through our childhood and beyond. I feel richer for having him back again, more whole.

I also came to recognize that in my teens, I had found the template, that of not allowing myself to feel painful feelings, that helped me to subsequently throw aside, like the dead fish they were to me, my first husband and later, Jean Claude. It helps, sometimes, to cast aside feeling, but such behavior also delays growth and development. I never really knew why I had left these two men. Not even Jean Claude's emotional abuse–his womanizing, his alcohol abuse –felt real to me. I never even confronted him about it. As for my husband, I returned to him after spending that first night with Jean Claude only to tell him where I'd been, to take my suitcase, and to leave him for what I knew was going to be forever. There was nothing to discuss, or so I believed. I knew that I would not change my mind as I had just experienced what I had felt to be "real" love with Jean Claude. All of this I have come to understand only because I was analyzed, an experience that has been life-changing for me.

If finding my father was a great psychoanalytic gift, having my mother materialize as a person, and not only as my mother, was another. My second analyst was at times relentless in exposing my defenses regarding my mother. As always, since my father's death, I was trying to protect and take care of her. It had become a habit, so much a part of me that I no more recognized it than I would recognize my own arm as being attached to my body. My second analyst penetrated my inner world where the anger lay, anger surrounding that woman who nursed me through infancy and then seemed dead to me, as she had in that old childhood nightmare of mine. It was the one in which I heard the sound of a gunshot ringing out from behind me as I tried to walk towards her, but I could only watch as she fell dead to the ground.

Yes, I was angry at her emotional neglect of me. She could not imagine that I was separate from her, a person with needs of my own that went unmet by her. But after many sessions of exploring this regurgitated anger and having it be received with empathy by my analyst, I saw my mother for the frightened woman she was. And I understood how, in her fear, she had clung to me, unable to give me what I needed to grow. Did her forgetting to feed me emotionally mean that she didn't love me enough? Was she jealous of my father's love for me? Probably. Was it her being depressed that made me feel she disliked me? She had no patience for caring for me in the way that a mother needs to care for her young child. Was it because she, herself, was feeling uncared for because my father left her, albeit in death? Or was it that the underlying anger that seems to go along with depression was wrongly targeted at me? The why of her lack of empathy and warmth towards me I can still only guess at, and I now feel that searching for an answer would be a waste of time.

With all of my anger gone, and with those unmet needs of my childhood having been so nakedly revealed in my second analysis, I can now see my mother more clearly. My anger, repressed as it was, finally gained a shape. My analyst came to understand those needs by being empathically attuned to me. They were then interpreted and worked and re-worked until I was able to find the best ways of getting my needs met by myself.

When I stopped being angry at my mother for having been unable to nurture me properly, I could see her for the person that she was–a good woman. She was particularly honest with herself and most other people. Honesty brought her to recognize her failures with me, and, in an effort at reparation, she tried to address them in ways that she could. She gave me her bed when I returned to America penniless, but she could not change her emotions. I knew that she had suffered, watching me flounder in my early adult life, and at the same time having to endure her own mother's silent criticism of her parenting. I think in some ways she continued to have anger towards me because I did not follow the path that she had expected of me, that of a conventional wife and mother, the life that she had chosen for herself that had got so tragically aborted. Yet when I did get engaged to my second husband, her initial response was one of happiness quickly followed by, "Are you sure you want to have a boss for the rest of your life?" Whatever her mixed messages were to me, I knew that my mother would never abandon me and would always be there if I were to fall.

She also tried her best to make her stepchildren happy and have something of a "normal" life, which they could not have had, given the critical father they had and the death, always unmentioned, of their own mother. My mother felt sorry for these children and wanted to brighten their lives, although her efforts failed.

Do I still suffer from anxiety? Of course. Who doesn't? I have a recurring dream of being lost while driving a car and trying to return home, or of not being able to find my way on the trains in a big city. There is always "How will I get home from wherever I have taken myself?" As I have travelled casually around Europe, more foolhardy than courageous, I accept these dreams as being partly PTSD, (post-traumatic stress disorder) anxiety that I could not feel at the time. Had I let myself experience those feelings, I would never have gone anywhere.

I have come to know myself better with age as well as with the aftereffects of psychoanalysis. I have learned that I am a little shy when meeting new people, more so as I have grown older, and that I cannot socialize for too long without longing to be alone again. I am content to recognize that I am, and probably always have been, an introvert. I realize now that the seemingly effortless socializing of my youth took place as long as I could lodge myself in the skirts of whomever I happened to be with at the time.

That I never had children of my own continues to be a loss for me. I sometimes mourn for what could have been, had I let myself have them. I felt unable to raise them alone. The various men I knew were unwilling partners in that regard. But now in my second marriage, I have two stepsons and they have given us grandchildren. The sons are in their early fifties and only now, after thirty years of being married to their father, am I claiming them as mine. I have been slow to embrace my position because they have their own very involved mother. Also, I believe, I too easily slipped into that slot of invisibility where I had spent a lot of my childhood being my "mother's assistant." As I outgrow that space, I claim what is mine. Things move slowly for me, but there is no doubt as to their certainty.

Does psychoanalysis make a person dependent on the analyst? This is a fear of anyone who is in therapy. My answer is that, for a time, it may, just as infants are dependent on their parents at the beginning of life, but as the old internal structures are being changed and re-made into new structures, according to Kohut through a process that he calls, "transmuting internalization," the result is that a self-sustaining adult has emerged.

Whether these structures have been acquired through a healthy and wholesome childhood or later during a successful analysis, natural needs must be either met or restored through appropriate empathy, validation, and encouragement. This growth process is what makes for a sense of security in adult life, a sense of confidence and self-esteem that enables the individual to go forward independently to meet his own needs. If attained through analysis, this constitutes a "cure."

I am a new/same person. I feel that I am the person I was meant to be, not the one I was in high school, college, Greece and France. My internal structure has changed as a result of giving up the old defenses that were there for self-protection. Giving them up left room for new growth. I was, then, able to recognize my own needs afresh. That is what psychoanalysis, and some other psychotherapies, can do. They can change us from the inside out. The pieces are moved around, discarded, or created anew.

Like life, psychoanalysis is a continuing process. It doesn't stop once we cease experiencing that flutter of expectation that occurs every time we ring the analyst's doorbell. Issues crop up, new feelings arise. But we are able to more quickly cut to the center of the matter, whatever it is, because we better understand ourselves and our emotions. We better understand what those feelings are telling us, and how to make use of them in an environment we have been able to choose for ourselves.

And so it goes.

ACKNOWLEDGMENTS

This book would not have been written had I not encountered people who, when they learned that I was a psychotherapist, told me their stories of failed attempts to get the therapy they needed. They urged me to write this book for them, for the people who had good intentions of going "to talk to someone" but whose intentions somehow got derailed.

I would like to thank my extraordinary editor Constance Rosenblum for her expertise mixed with intelligence, kindness, patience, and unwavering enthusiasm for the book. I would also like to thank Jonnet Abeles and Rosemary Steinbaum. Jonnet, known as the "Comma Momma"—and so much more—never faltered in her commitment to getting this book launched. Rosemary's intelligent read caused me to reformulate certain ideas in the book. I thank them all for their generous help.

I also want to thank my valuable colleagues and friends for their time and their warm response to my writing: Lisa Sokoloff, Susan Goldman, Eva Stark, Sandy Rzetelny, Naomi Fox, Ed Ross, Ashley Warner, Steven Kuchuck and Penny Rosen—all of whom rushed to help.

I belong to a writers' group in the Northern Adirondacks whose members corrected and supported me through writes and rewrites. Thank you Noel Mzese, Beckie O'Neill , Yvona Fast, Ann Mullen, Liz DeFonce, and Amy Bowers who did a great job in getting the manuscript into a computer file, and my friend Caperton Tisssot who never faltered in her belief in me and the book.

I had a "family tech team" whose help I enlisted to compensate for my computer ineptness. My niece, Leslie Cohen, was always patiently at the other end of the phone while figuring out how to advise me, as were my stepsons, Jon and Jeff Kolsky.

And lastly, I want to thank my remarkable husband who helped me in so many different ways from correcting grammar to providing unlimited love and unwavering support—and who now says that he will divorce me if I write another book.